Mount Hermon Libraries

MOUNT HERMON ◆ MASSACHUSETTS

Arms Control

Arms Control

Theory and Practice

Michael Sheehan

Basil Blackwell

Copyright © Michael Sheehan 1988

First published 1988

Basil Blackwell Ltd
108 Cowley Road, Oxford OX4 1JF, UK

Basil Blackwell Inc.
432 Park Avenue South, Suite 1503
New York, NY 10016, USA

British Library Cataloguing in Publication Data
Sheehan, Michael
   Arms control: theory and practice.
   1. Arms control
   I. Title
   327.1'74   JX1974

   ISBN 0-631-14164-2
   ISBN 0-631-16059-0 Pbk

Library of Congress Cataloging in Publication Data
Sheehan, Michael J.
   Arms control.

   Includes index.
   1. Arms control. I. Title.
JX1974.S473   1988   327.1'74
87-30945
ISBN 0-631-14164-2
ISBN 0-631-16059-0 (pbk.)

Typeset in 10 on 12pt Baskerville
by Downdell Ltd., Abingdon, Oxon.
Printed in Great Britain by Billing & Sons Ltd, Worcester

Contents

Preface

On 8 December 1987 US President Ronald Reagan and General Secretary Mikhail Gorbachev signed the INF Treaty in Washington. The treaty involved the elimination of 1286 nuclear missiles from Europe and Asia, and over 2,000 nuclear warheads. The agreement involved the most comprehensive and stringent verification procedures ever seen in an arms control treaty. Perhaps most significantly, the treaty breathed new life into the comatose superpower arms control process.

The attainment of the treaty threw into sharp relief the post-war arms control record, for the agreement was the first bilateral superpower arms control treaty signed since 1979, the first to undergo the full process of Senate ratification since the SALT I agreement of 1972, and only the second agreement since 1945 to abolish and prohibit an entire category of weapons. Welcome as the INF Treaty was to the public and the arms control community, it nonetheless highlighted the dismal record of arms control since its inception in the later 1950s. A number of questions are raised by this record. Why has arms control achieved so little? What are the impediments, domestic and international, which have so limited its impact? Is the arms control process itself fatally flawed or can the obstacles to success be overcome?

The objective of this book is to address these questions, to look at the way in which superpower arms control has been pursued to date and the difficulties it has encountered. In doing so the book attempts not only to throw light upon the very real problems which have hindered progress in the past, but also to enable the reader to judge the extent to which the revival of detente in the later 1980s and the greater flexibility of the post-*glasnost* Soviet Union offers the possibility of the attainment of significant breakthroughs in arms control in the 1990s.

Abbreviations

ABM	Anti-Ballistic Missile
ACDA	Arms Control and Disarmament Agency
ASAT	Anti-Satellite
BMD	Ballistic Missile Defence
CTB	Comprehensive Test Ban
GDP	Gross Domestic Product
GNP	Gross National Product
ICBM	Intercontinental Ballistic Missile
INF	Intermediate Nuclear Forces
LTBT	Limited Test Ban Treaty
MBFR	Mutual and Balanced Force Reduction talks
MIRV	Multiple Independently Targeted Re-entry Vehicle
MX	Missile Experimental (now called Peacekeeper)
NATO	North Atlantic Treaty Organization
NPT	Non-Proliferation Treaty
NTM	National Technical Means
OSI	On-Site Inspection
PNET	Peaceful Nuclear Explosions Treaty
SALT	Strategic Arms Limitation Treaty
SDI	Strategic Defence Initiative
SIOP	Single Integrated Operational Plan
SLBM	Submarine Launched Ballistic Missile
SLCM	Submarine Launched Cruise Missile
SSBN	Strategic Submarine, Ballistic, Nuclear
START	Strategic Arms Reduction Talks
TGWU	Transport and General Workers' Union
TTBT	Threshold Test-Ban Treaty
WTO	Warsaw Treaty Organization

1

The Origins of Arms Control

Arms control is essentially a means of supplementing unilateral military strategy by some kind of collaboration with the countries that are potential enemies. The aims of arms control and the aims of a national military strategy should be substantially the same.

Schelling and Halperin, Strategy and Arms Control[1]

Introduction

Any attempt to analyse the achievements, failures and problems of the arms control record of the past 25 years must begin by looking at the meaning and purpose of arms control. This may seem obvious but in fact it is very rarely done. Almost from its inception commentators have tended to use 'arms control' as a synonym for disarmament and to then judge arms control by the degree of disarmament occurring at any particular time. In fact, however, there are crucial differences in the meaning and approach of arms control and disarmament and the failure to appreciate this accounts for some (but by no means all) of the disillusionment with the arms control approach which has manifested itself in the past few years.

Arms control is *not* the same thing as disarmament, though the two approaches are not mutually exclusive. In order to set the arms control record in its proper context, therefore, it is necessary to go back to the nativity of the arms control approach and look again at what its framers said it was and, which is equally important, what it was not. The arms control approach emerged partly in response to the advent of the nuclear 'balance of terror' and partly as a response to a perceived failure of the disarmament approach in the years immediately before and after the Second World War. To appreciate, why the arms control approach emerged when it did it is worth glancing at the experience of the post-war years before going on to look at the difference between arms control and disarmament and the methods and problems associated with the arms control approach.

The Failure of Disarmament 1945–1955

The military and political realities of the post-war era produced a number of often conflicting pressures within the international system. On the one hand there was a palpable war-weariness which produced a general desire, particularly in the West, to disarm and demobilize as rapidly and as comprehensively as possible once the war was over. Against this desire to disarm was ranged the onset of the Cold War, which developed inexorably between 1946 and 1948 and culminated in the Berlin blockade, the Czechoslovak Coup and, in 1949, the formation of NATO. Despite these events the Western states were exceedingly reluctant to begin rearming and were only triggered into a major military build-up by the outbreak of the Korean War in 1950. Soviet demobilization was much slower than that in the West, impeded by a fear of German revanchism, the threat posed by the US nuclear monopoly and the manpower demands of the need to garrison the Soviet-dominated buffer zone being created in Eastern Europe. Even so a steady demobilization of Soviet forces also took place during this period, though it did not match the pace of reductions in the West.

However, 1945 had changed the whole context of the debate about disarmament. Nuclear weapons had been used in war and could not be disinvented. The awesome potential for catastrophe which nuclear weapons represented increased the general desire for disarmament but at the same time placed major new obstacles in the path of effective disarmament. Disarmament agreements had been difficult enough to negotiate prior to 1945, but in the nuclear era the implications of war and of poorly drafted or unilaterally broken agreements had become even more profound. The consequences of successful cheating by a nuclear-armed state might mean literal annihilation for the state or states that were its victims. Against this, the difficulties involved in negotiating massive disarmament involving nuclear and non-nuclear adversaries were enormous, as the fate of the Baruch Plan showed.

In November 1946, 15 months after the nuclear attack on Japan, the US submitted a plan for the elimination of all nuclear weapons. This proposal became known as the 'Baruch Plan', after Bernard Baruch, one of its authors. Under the plan the US, at that time the only state in the world possessing nuclear weapons, offered to dismantle them and make its civil nuclear knowledge available to other states. Weapons disposal and peaceful nuclear energy programmes were to be supervised by a new International Atomic Development Authority created for that purpose. The UN General Assembly adopted the plan on 31 December 1946 but the proposal was rejected by the Soviet Union and its allies. The Soviet Union objected to the 'control before disarmament' approach advocated by the US. The Baruch Plan called for the establishment of the monitoring and supervision agency before disarmament began. The Soviets were suspicious of the pro-Western majority the organization would have and felt that the Authority would be able to prevent Soviet research into nuclear weapons whereas US scientists had already acquired the knowledge needed to construct them. From a Soviet perspective, therefore, the plan seemed to confer a permanent advantage upon the US. Although the US criticized the Soviet attitude at the time, it is noticeable that after 1949, when the Soviet Union exploded its first atomic bomb, the US became prey to a similar lack of confidence in the idea of international control of nuclear weapons. After the Soviet H-bomb test in 1954 the US abandoned the idea completely.

The Baruch Plan was important because it represented probably the last chance to achieve a complete ban on nuclear weapons. During the 1950s the superpowers continued to call for such a ban, and indeed for the total abolition of all weapons of any magnitude, but these calls represented little more than propagandist posturing. They were designed for public consumption, not as a basis for negotiation. It was, however, politically dangerous to go too far in ridiculing the other side's schemes. In 1951 Britain and France submitted a disarmament proposal which called for inspection of armaments followed by unspecified reductions at a later date. The proposal as formulated was guaranteed to prove indigestible for the Soviet Union, and indeed the Soviet UN ambassador Vishinsky scoffed at it, saying it had kept him awake all night laughing. The result was a propaganda catastrophe for the Soviet Union. Public opinion in the West and the developing world was outraged and posters appeared showing a world dissolving in flames with Vishinski in the form of a hyena, laughing at the destruction.[2]

During the 1950s it gradually became clear that complete nuclear disarmament was no longer possible. The crucial issue was the question of the verification of compliance with a total ban. The French government were the first to argue publicly that a total ban was impossible on the grounds that the amount of fissile material in existence had reached the point where no verification system could be produced which could absolutely guarantee that none had been hidden. Total nuclear disarmament would therefore demand total trust of the other side, and that degree of trust did not exist in the Cold War and was an impossible objective to pursue. The French took the logical stance that since a total ban was no longer possible the honest approach would be for the major powers to stop pretending that they were actively seeking such a ban. The French were absolutely right, but it was to be several years before the superpowers could bring themselves to admit that this was indeed the case.[3]

The verification impasse continued to bedevil disarmament negotiations as the 1950s unfolded. The Soviet Union viewed its secretive society as a military asset and was unwilling to surrender this advantage.[4] The West saw satisfactory verification as an absolute necessity in any agreement. The gap between the two sides' basic positions proved impossible to close.

In 1955 it could at last be said that arms control began to displace disarmament as the realistic goal of the superpowers. In that year the Soviet Union and US admitted for the first time that they no longer saw complete nuclear disarmament as a feasible goal of diplomacy. In May 1955 the Soviet Union submitted a new disarmament proposal which confessed that 'there are possibilities beyond the reach of international control for circumventing this control and organising the secret manufacture of atomic and hydrogen weapons, even if there is a formal agreement of international control.'[5] The Soviet proposal concentrated instead upon the gains to be made for international security from constraining each side's potential for launching a surprise attack.

These two ideas, the impossibility of a total nuclear ban and the need to deter surprise attack, were central pillars of the US academic arms control approach in later years. The Soviet ideas undoubtedly chimed with the evolving US position and in August of the same year the US itself adopted a similar stance, rescinding all its previous disarmament proposals and declaring that production of fissionable materials had passed the point where it could all be satisfactorily accounted for.[6] The US argued that diplomatic energies should instead be focused upon stabilizing the balance of power and reducing the temptation to initiate war. Eisenhower's 'Open Skies' proposal at the 1955 summit meeting grew out of the new way of thinking, namely that the balance of nuclear power should be safeguarded and stabilized rather than abolished.

By the time this position was reached a profound scepticism about the general possibilities for disarmament had set in. Fifteen years of effort since 1945 had failed to produce a single formal agreement. Moreover, while the popular desire for disarmament remained,, governments on both sides of the East–West divide were more sanguine. A belief that disarmament efforts in the inter-war years had not prevented the Second World War, and indeed might have aided Hitler's advance, left governments cautious about disarmament. Nuclear weapons were now seen as an ultimate deterrent upon which a stable power balance could be built.

The years of negotiations after 1945 had not been entirely wasted. They had produced a limited consensus between the superpowers over both the dangers of nuclear war and the potential stabilizing effect of a nuclear balance of power. Neither side wanted to abandon its nuclear deterrent and both realized that public opinion expected continuing negotiations on the arms issues, and expected such negotiations to be conducted in good faith. The superpowers were therefore driven to recognize that the depth of their political antagonism, which ruled out the degree of trust necessary for disarmament but not the danger of nuclear war, compelled them to explore their common interest in avoiding a mutual catastrophe.

Differences between Arms Control and Disarmament

Between 1957 and 1962 the strategic community in the US spelled out what they meant by the arms control approach and the ways in which it differed from traditional disarmament. A representative definition was that of Bowie:

> The concept of 'arms control' includes any agreement among several powers to regulate some aspect of their military capability or potential. The arrangement may apply to the location, amount, readiness, or types of military forces, weapons or facilities.[7]

This definition, while useful, omits the crucial point noted in Schelling and Halperin, that the cooperation is between potential adversaries.[8] In a famous formulation they included in arms control any kind of military cooperation between potential enemies with the aim of 'reducing the likelihood of war; its scope and violence if it occurs, and the political and economic costs of being prepared for it'.[9] Schelling wrote elsewhere of arms control allowing collaboration with her enemies in order to improve the military posture of the US.[10]

Whereas disarmament was seen as an alternative to military strength, arms control was seen as a complement to it, since both were different ways of enhancing national and international security.[11] Arms control was felt to represent a recognition of the continuing utility of military power in the modern world.[12] Unlike proponents of disarmament, who saw the existence of weapons as a cause of arms races and war, the new arms controllers believed that there was no simple cause and effect relationship between the possession of weapons and the outbreak of war. Armaments, it was argued, were ever-present features in the landscape of international politics and were as much a part of the peacetime as of the wartime environment.[13]

Many of the new arms control community were overtly contemptuous of the disarmament approach, calling it 'a tragic illusion, if not a deliberate fraud'.[14] Even those who were less disparaging were equally dismissive, arguing that most people were sceptical of the prospects for disarmament and 'such cynicism is strongly supported by historical precedents.'[15] Disarmament, it was felt, demanded so many unrealistic assumptions that negotiations were doomed from the start.[16] Indeed Spanier and Nogee argued that far from being a way out of the arms race, superpower disarmament negotiations were in fact simply another form of it, the aim of both being to obtain an exploitable margin of relative power over the adversary.[17]

Not all arms controllers saw disarmament and arms control as distinct and incompatible with one another. There was a school of thought which argued that arms control was a generic term, covering any arrangement designed to reduce the likelihood of international military conflict and ranging from unilateral national force improve-ments at one end of the spectrum of possibilities to universal disarma-ment at the other.[18]

Nevertheless, most of the writers on arms control were at pains to distinguish between the two approaches, both because they felt that there were crucial differences between the two and because they had specific misgivings about the implications of major nuclear disarma-ment. The crucial distinguishing feature separating arms control from disarmament was that disarmament always involves arms reductions. These reductions might be total, involving the abolition of all arms; they might mean the abolition of one *type* of weapon; they might be partial, involving numerical reductions in some or all categories of weapons; or they might be local, regional or global. Reduction, however, was the key.

Arms control in contrast *may* involve reductions, but need not necessarily do so. Indeed, in certain circumstances the arms control approach produces a requirement for more, not fewer, weapons. The disarmament approach assumes that weapons are a cause of war, therefore to abolish weapons is to abolish war. The arms control approach believes that wars begin in the minds of men, that peace and stability are as much a function of intentions as they are of military capabilities. If states wish to fight they will find the means to do so. The objective thus becomes the control of those factors which prompt states to go to war, of which the greatest is fear: fear of the intentions of a potential adversary, fear that the political situation is getting out of control, and fear of the implications of certain weapon systems. The way to overcome these fears is to construct an inter-national political environment in which a stable balance of power exists with neither side significantly disadvantaged by it and in which neither is tempted to attack by the weakness of the other. Such an environment requires a high degree of 'military transparency' so that the legitimate defensive preparations of each side can be seen for what they are and secretive military movements or deployments do not trigger fear of attack. It is an environment where the existence of a military balance is seen as a stabilizing factor, a good thing, but where it is recognized that some weapons or deployments might threaten this stability and where therefore there exists a common interest in creating a negotiated environment which minimizes or even eliminates the destabilizing influences of certain new technologies or strategies.

The operational result of these basic assumptions is that arms controllers aim to discriminate between 'those kinds and quantities of forces and weapons that promote the stability of the balance of power, and those which do not; to tolerate or even to promote the former, and to restrict the latter'.[19]

In disarmament, therefore, an increase in weaponry is always bad. In the arms control approach this is not so. This difference has all sorts of implications, which are analysed throughout this book, but some of them are worth noting at this point because they were central tenets for the original arms controllers which have largely been lost sight of in the subsequent public debate.

One key feature is the acceptance of nuclear deterrence. The new arms controllers did not see deterrence as an immoral expedient to be abandoned as soon as was practically possible. On the contrary, they saw nuclear weapons as an innovation that might well make war between the great powers impossible. To abolish nuclear weapons would thus be a retrograde step. Nuclear deterrence was to be the 'keystone' of national security, something to be enhanced and refined through measures to make it less accident-prone and to safeguard each side's retaliatory capability. Stable new weapon systems such as submarine launched ballistic missiles (SLBMs) were to be welcomed, not feared.

This outlook conflicted with the idea that arms control was a kind of modest disarmament. There always existed a minority within the arms control community who reflected a more prevalent perception among the general public, that arms control was disarmament in easy stages. President Kennedy's Science Adviser saw arms control in this way, arguing that arms control would make possible the eventual elimination of all military forces through a series of incremental reductions;[20] but this was to miss the point constantly reiterated by the early proponents, that arms control, while aiming to preserve a balance of power founded upon guaranteed retaliatory capability, could hardly be interpreted as simply another route towards ultimate disarmament.[21] Arms control was in fundamental opposition to the whole ethos of disarmament since it concerned the strengthening of the balance of military power. It was concerned neither with reductions *per se* nor with indiscriminate attempts to interfere either with quantitative or qualitative increases in weaponry.

This difference in aim was compounded by suspicions about the desirability of disarmament, even in the unlikely event that it could be achieved. Disarmament was seen as Utopian because it demanded improvements in human and state behaviour patterns that – on even the most optimistic assumptions – were not likely to materialize in the foreseeable future. Disarmament would be possible only within 'a new context, involving basic changes in world politics',[22] the fundamental requirement being the emergence of a world government, superseding the nation-state, capable of supervising and maintaining the disarmament process. A world government of this sort was seen as being out of the question for generations to come.

In the absence of such a supervisory authority the alternative was disarmament managed and operated by nation-states themselves, and the new thinkers of the late 1950s held grave doubts as to the essential stability of an unarmed, multinational world.[23] In a disarmed world the advantages of cheating would be enormously magnified since even a small hidden arsenal would represent a weapons monopoly. Even if force levels were merely reduced to very low levels rather than being completely abolished, this incentive to cheat would remain. The arms controllers argued that the absolute level of weaponry was as crucial to stability as the ratios involved. Since small forces were more vulnerable to marginal advantages on each side, it was better for stability if parity were maintained at high rather than low levels, since then marginal differences would have no practical significance. Beyond a certain point, therefore, arms reductions were seen as increasing the likelihood of war, a crucial point of departure from the disarmament approach. The arms controllers thus sought 'a goal well short of the complete elimination of strategic weapons'.[24] In fact not only was arms control concerned to retain such weapons, it preferred to retain them in very large numbers.

Arms control was therefore a very different exercise from disarmament, with goals for which balanced reductions in weapons totals were not only sometimes irrelevant, but were occasionally inimical. Yet in public discourse, in academic writings as much as government statements, the terms 'disarmament' and 'arms control' continued to be used as if they were the same thing,[25] and as the term 'disarmament' faded from government parlance 'arms control' came to be seen as a synonym for the same objective.

This confusion was to lead to public disillusion during the 1970s as governments stabilized the nuclear balance of power, thereby achieving the major goal of arms control, but did this by way of building up their weapons rather than reducing them, leaving the public feeling it was being deliberately ignored in its wish for arms reductions. For governments control meant control: even mutually agreed increases represents control compared to unregulated arms races. For the general public 'control' means arms freezes at worst, arms reductions at best.

In the early 1960s the arms control community was not unresponsive to this popular preference. Reductions were seen as being worthy of pursuit, *in so far as they did not threaten stability*. For a variety of reasons, however, it was to be many years before it was felt that the deterrent relationship was stable enough to encompass major reductions, and by that time a variety of factors were bearing upon the arms control negotiating process in such a way as to make it extremely difficult to achieve the tolerable reductions. One remarkable feature of the writings from the 'golden years' of arms control theorizing (1957–62) is the perceptiveness with which many of the problems that came to shackle arms control were foreseen. Before looking at these, however, it is necessary to look at the purpose envisaged for arms control and the methods which were deemed appropriate for achieving it, for once again the subsequent practice has differed in crucial ways from the original theory.

The Purpose and Methods of Arms Control

The essential objective of arms control is to make the world safe for nuclear deterrence. It assumes that nuclear weapons cannot be eliminated and that the world must therefore learn to live with them.[26] While the nuclear balance of terror is seen as a positive development it is not assumed that this balance will maintain itself; constant care and fine-tuning are required if the stability of the balance is to be continuously maintained, and while unilateral initiatives can play a part in achieving this end, negotiations with the potential adversary are a crucial element. While numerically high

balances were seen as stabilizing, there was nevertheless a recogn
that a great deal of each superpower's military effort simply cancell
out the efforts of the other side, and that therefore there existed a
common interest in determining whether or not mutual deterrence
might be attainable at lower levels of deployments and expenditure.
While it was felt that controls of some description were clearly
preferable to an unrestrained arms race, it was also recognized that
the control process itself involved a measure of risk, since one's own
unilateral capabilities were restrained while verification uncertainties
would leave a possibility that the other side was less constrained. It
was important, therefore, that any arms control reduce the danger of
the arms race by more than the scale of risk produced by the control
itself. A marginal security gain of this sort was seen as being the best
that arms control could hope for.[27]

Whereas disarmament could only be achieved in a world much
changed from our own, arms control did not need to wait for
improvements in the international environment; on the contrary, 'it
is only in the presence of political disputes and tensions serious
enough to generate arms competitions that arms control has any
relevance.'[28] This was a crucial issue, for while it was true to say that
political tension need not be an obstacle to arms control in the way
that it was for disarmament, nevertheless (as the experience of the
subsequent 25 years showed all too clearly) arms control would
remain a hostage to the degree of *détente* present at any particular
time. Some degree of *détente* needs to be present to allow arms control
negotiations to progress, but this will not necessarily prevent such
efforts being derailed by crises, unrelated to arms control, occurring
elsewhere in the international system. This problem is looked at in
chapters 5 and 6.

The early writings on arms control also addressed the tangential
gains which arms control might make possible. One purpose of arms
control talks, it was suggested, would be 'to educate the Soviets in
mutually desirable strategies and armament policies'.[29] Experience
demonstrated that this was to be a less straightforward task than it
seemed in 1960 and that the educative process would by no means be
simply one-way traffic.

Arms control, it was felt, might also have a beneficial impact upon
superpower relations generally, not just the military–strategic
relationship. If adversaries could develop the habit of mutually

ition in an area of their relations as fraught with
...tegic balance, then this habit of cooperation might
...her areas. It might then act as a catalyst for the
...al problems. The Kissinger–Nixon period of *détente*
...:o validate this thesis to some extent, but at the same
...ited the vulnerabilities of the approach.

...ose of arms control was inherited from the disarmament approach. A major function, probably *the* major function of
arms negotiations, is not so much to arrive at an agreement as to be
seen by public opinion to be trying to reach an agreement. It is also
crucial to place the onus for failure to reach agreement upon the other
side. Arms control represented an advance upon disarmament in this
respect. Although governments on both sides were still not overwhelmingly bothered whether they reached agreement or not, nevertheless the difference in essential approach coupled with the more
modest goals of arms control meant that governments were far more
inclined to accept an agreement if they could get one. This presup-
posed an agreement upon their own terms, of course.[30]

It remained the case, however, that an acceptable deal would have
to meet very demanding criteria. If it did not enhance strategic
stability it was not worth doing. There was no sense, as there was for
proponents of disarmament, that the activity was good for its own
sake. If other benefits flowed from it, so much the better, but unless a
deal enhanced stability it should be rejected.[31] Stability was the *sine
qua non* of the arms control exercise. It was what made the balance of
terror acceptable and, for the arms controllers, 'proposals to abolish
the "terror" in the "balance of terror" are clearly out of order.'[32]
Schelling and Halperin maintained, however, that the greater the
stability the less terror the situation would hold, since the terror was a
function of the instability. Attempts to stabilize deterrence therefore
represented 'efforts to tranquilize anxieties'.[33] Certainly arms control
efforts over the past 30 years can be seen in this light as a sedative
designed to make bearable the public's nuclear *angst*.

In proposing methods to achieve arms control the early theorists
took a much broader view than subsequent history would lead one to
expect. As early as 1960 Hedley Bull made the point that formal
treaties were only one of a number of ways in which arms control
might be achieved; but treaties are not essential to arms control.[34]
Other methods would include executive agreements, explicit but

informal understandings, and 'self-restraint that is consciously contingent on each other's behaviour'.[35]

Around 1960, when these ideas were being formulated, the record of formal negotiated agreements was virtually non-existent, the only minor success being the 1959 Antarctic Treaty. It was ironic that one of the coldest places on earth should provide evidence of a thaw in superpower relations. A freeze on deployment proved harder to reach in sunnier climes. Given the limited success of formal negotiations it was not surprising that the arms controllers emphasized the value of informal techniques and even of unilateral initiatives. Lefever, for example, argued that 'mutual restraint can lead to tacit understandings that are in many ways as effective as formal agreements.'[36] Schelling and Halperin spoke of 'induced or reciprocated "self-control"' to convey the same meaning.[37]

One way in which the definition of arms control has narrowed over time is that one further arms control technique is no longer automatically associated with the approach. In the late 1950s it was argued that unilateral efforts to improve one's own military force posture in such a way as to facilitate second-strike capabilities constituted arms control as much as would a test-ban treaty, since both enhanced stability.[38] Nowadays it would be a brave government that based its sole claim to progress in arms control on the additional deployment of mobile single-warhead missiles, or city-busting submarine-launched missiles, yet this would be perfectly consistent with the original meaning of arms control. It can be argued that the deployment of Polaris and Yankee-class SSBNs did more for world peace in the 1960s and 1970s than any of the negotiated arms control agreements.

The arms controllers in 1960 were also far more sympathetic to unilateral moves than has subsequently been the case, with Schelling suggesting that 'instead of arguing about what we should do we . . . simply do it and dare the other side to do likewise.'[39] As a variant of this it was suggested that the US take limited initiatives and quietly make it known to the Soviet Union what reciprocal measures would cause the US to continue its restraint. Jerome Weisner, however, was less confident of the value of unilateral actions, arguing that significant unilateral actions would be destablizing in a way that negotiated bilateral restraints would not.[40]

One proposal which certainly was acted upon subsequently (though largely because of the trauma of the Cuban Missile Crisis) was the suggestion that 'The arms race might be damped if each side possessed better information about what the other side is doing.'[41] This was felt to be true not only with regard to reducing the threat-assessment errors produced by 'worst-case' analysis, but also in terms of reducing the dangers of unintended nuclear war by establishing communication procedures, information exchanges and possibly reciprocal inspection facilities. With regard to the latter, it was noted that the greater the confidence in the verification measures available, the lower could be the level of weaponry deemed to be prudent for stability.[42]

Many, if not most, of the other proposed techniques put forward at this time were acted upon to some extent during the subsequence 25 years. The European–American Assembly in 1961 called for technical constraints upon nuclear weapon capabilities, controls on delivery systems, controls on fissile materials, efforts to ban nuclear weapons from outer space and measures to give greater assurance against surprise attack, technical accident and miscalculation. All these approaches were tried during the 1960s and 1970s. As well as mapping out the promising directions for arms control, the Western advocates of the late 1950s were also remarkably prescient in anticipating the problems likely to be encountered by the arms control process.

Problems Facing Arms Control

It was recognized from an early stage that arms control measures were likely to be cautious and conservative because they represented such a break with traditional military practice. Disarmament presupposes a high degree of amity and trust. Arms control was meant to take place between states with a profound mistrust and hostility towards one another and there is nothing traditional about military collaboration between potential enemies. The fact that both sides could recognize a common interest in avoiding mutual nuclear annihilation did not mean that they would be able to move from that basic recognition to the achievement of practical cooperation for the purpose of limiting their competition.

Moreover, even if limited arms control measures could be negotiated there was the problem of how to insulate the negotiations and agreements from the consequences of conflicts between the bargaining partners occuring in other areas. Clearly problems would arise from differing perceptions of what kinds of behaviour in other areas were compatible with the new relationship the arms control agreement was held to create. Schelling and Halperin, analysing potential difficulties in 1961, might almost have been describing the actual course of superpower relations in the mid-1970s when they wrote:

> The least favourable prognosis is probably for an agreement that one party expects to symbolize the burying of the hatchet, a new era of good feeling, and a resolution to live up to new standards of international friendship, while the other takes for granted that 'realistic' diplomacy will prevail, subject only to the concrete matters agreed on. In this case acute disappointment and recrimination might result, and the greatest of misunderstandings.[43]

The same authors predicted another problem likely to arise with the arms control method, the 'substitution' effect looked at in chapter 5. Since arms control discriminates between certain military programmes which are condoned and others which are constrained, there is a strong likelihood that when certain weapon systems are limited, each side will look for other ways of doing the task formerly performed by the constrained weaponry. The Soviet Union, for example, complained that US cruise missile deployments in Europe after 1983 were a way of getting round the SALT II limits on the number of nuclear warheads targeted on each side's homeland.

Henry Kissinger drew attention in the early 1960s to the fact that there were certain implicit assumptions in the arms control approach and one of them was the assumption that there would exist an agreed strategic doctrine. Without such a doctrine arms control would not be possible because there would be no criteria against which to judge whether a weapon or programme would increase or decrease stability.[44] This problem has bedevilled the superpower arms control relationship and proved particularly divisive during the arguments over the desirability of ballistic missile defences, (BMD) in the late 1960s and mid-1980s.

As well as criteria against which to measure possible arms control initiatives there was also a need to be able to decide priorities between arms control objectives when these were in conflict. As the arms control approach developed in the late 1950s various objectives were called for, such as reducing the risks of war, reducing the costs of being prepared for war and so on. It would not always be possible to reconcile these objectives: for example, 'hardening' missile silos to make them less vulnerable to surprise attack would reduce the risk of war, but increase the cost of preparing for it. BMD might reduce the death and destruction involved if war broke out, but would increase defence costs, and increase the danger of war breaking out in the first place.

Considerations of this sort led arms controllers to look at the economic implications of arms control and disarmament and to try to assess their relative impact. It was decided early on that, to achieve the goals of stability, economic gains from arms control would be limited. This question is addressed in chapter 4. It is worth stressing that in general terms the arms control community in this formative period was very careful to emphasize what arms control could *not* achieve as much as what it could. It would be unfair to blame them, therefore, for the exaggerated expectations of arms control potential which became common in the 1970s for example. A typically cautious note was that struck by Schelling and Halperin, namely that while sensible arms control measures might reduce East–West tensions and thereby allay some of the dangers inherent in the Cold War, 'it is certainly too much to hope that arms control by its very inauguration will end the Cold War.'[45]

The intrinsic difficulties of constraining the technological arms race were also fully appreciated. Henry Kissinger drew attention to the crucial importance of identifying potentially destabilizing systems while they were still at an early stage of development and before the emergence of a coalition of vested interests favouring their deployment.[46] Kissinger himself was to have a mixed record when it came to following his own advice while in office.[47] The problem of trying to identify likely technological threats at an early stage was that it meant trying to control arms at a point where their likely implications were far from being clear.

This would prove to be a continuous problem. It is in the nature of politics that governments tend to become active only when issues become politically critical. It is hard to sustain interest in issues that may be complex, time-consuming and of little obvious political benefit. Yet change itself is something which is continuous. A difficulty noted by Hedley Bull in 1961 was that while politicians and military experts are aware of the idea of change and technological progress, they are often only dimly alive to its essential continuity.[48] They become fascinated by the strategic potential of some new technology and come to see it as a final technological solution to problems. Yet these are merely episodes in the history of technology; there can be no final solutions as such. It was notable in the 1980s, for example, that the Reagan administration, while extolling the virtues of SDI as a solution to the problem of ballistic missiles, failed to appreciate that technological advance would occur beyond SDI in both offensive and defensive technologies, so that SDI would accelerate a combined offence–defence arms race but could not 'solve' the nuclear arms race in any definitive sense. Technology does not remain static, and neither does scientific advance routinely favour defence over offence, or vice versa. The relationship is always dynamic. Bull noted that there were very clear limits to what arms control could achieve in terms of restraining technology. Continuous innovation was a notable feature of defence industries, but more significantly it was characteristic of modern industrial society generally and there was not the slightest chance of this being reversed in the foreseeable future.[49]

Controlling military technology was made still more difficult by the fact that the armed forces of each side rely on different 'mixes' of weapons and men to provide their security. It would be almost inevitable, therefore, that limitations on any particular weapon system would affect one treaty partner more than another, making it more difficult to reach agreement.[50] Moreover, each side is likely to be ahead in some areas of military technology and behind in others, making an agreement which constrained both sides equally a complex objective. The obstacles produced by this would be increased by the tendency of each side's military experts to feel that any proposed constraint was likely to affect them more than the adversary. Each side invariably exaggerates its own deficiencies while minimizing those of the other side. With this lack of confidence in the ability to predict the actual impact of constraint on each side, any agreements reached would be marked by their caution and conservatism.[51]

Even after an agreement had been concluded, technological advances would continue to threaten the deal by altering the impact of constraints on each side and thereby the relative costs and benefits.[52] This clearly would lead to suspicion that one side had anticipated these changes and effectively tricked the other into concluding an agreement that was not genuinely in its interests. Even when technologies are limited, the military by seeking alternative, unconstrained routes to achieve the former objectives will continuously threaten to disrupt the stability achieved by the agreement.[53] Certainly in the 1970s the effects of the SALT treaties in limiting launcher totals was undermined by the development of multiple warheads and cruise missiles.

The essential feature stressed by the arms controllers was that arms control was a technically-oriented solution to what was actually a political problem, and this had to be constantly borne in mind.[54]

Henry Kissinger linked technological and political change to the negotiation process, pointing out that arms control structures would be just as prone to obsolescence as the technologies and strategies they dealt with. They would therefore need integral mechanisms for adaptation and review.[55] This was an observation that has tended to become lost in subsequent years where certain treaties have acquired the status of holy writ and are treated as if any suggested amendment would produce the collapse of the entire edifice. Review processes have been rather more successful, particularly the Standing Consultative Commission established for the SALT treaties.

The early arms control community's attitudes towards the negotiating process was in fact strongly influenced by observation of the post-war disarmament negotiations. It was recognized that many arms control offers would be propaganda gestures rather than genuine attempts to reach agreement. It was also accepted that it would be extremely difficult to overcome the negative Cold War images each side held of the other, which meant the other side's proposals would never be taken at face value but always examined for a hidden, 'real' purpose.[56]

Cold War attitudes were not always absent from the arms control community itself. Concern was expressed, for example, that the democratic alliances should not allow themselves to be lulled into a state of complacency by the habit of cooperation with the adversary. There was a fear that Western public opinion would view arms control agreements as a sign that military effort could be reduced and perhaps the alliances themselves dismantled.[57] This fear resurfaced at intervals during the next 20 years, inspired by the neutralist murmurings of certain European opposition parties.

The tension between the need for arms control effort and the danger of its anaesthetic effect could not be avoided, however. It was accepted that public opinion would not tolerate governments which made no effort to achieve progress in arms control and that public support for necessary military effort would probably not be forthcoming to governments which appeared to be indifferent to the dangers of the arms race.

At the same time the central purpose of arms control needed to be borne in mind. The aim was to increase military stability rather than seek other ends, and collateral gains from arms control negotiations would be insufficient compensation if the agreements themselves were poorly conceived.[58] This goal was certainly lost sight of during the interminable MBFR negotiations on European conventional forces.

Major breakthroughs were not seen as being always necessary, however. The rationale of the SALT 'process' of successive agreements was foreshadowed by, for example, Schelling and Halperin, who argued that specific arms control deals might be desirable because, while marginal in their impact, they paved the way for further agreements (though poor agreements might be counterproductive in this respect). Limited agreements would also make possible the evaluation of techniques necessary for more comprehensive agreements.[59] Certainly some subsequent agreements such as the Threshold Test Ban Treaty (TTBT), and Peaceful Nuclear Explosions Treaty (PNET) of the 1970s were useful not so much for their specific constraints as for the breakthrough in verification techniques which they represented.

Verification itself was immediately recognized as being the greatest potential obstacle to successful arms control. The inherent distrust of Cold War relationships led to a need for verification while making that verification extremely difficult to achieve. The essential elements of the verification debate were clearly present in the early arms control writings, but there were signs even then of the differences in outlook over what would constitute adequate verification, which were to become so marked in the 1970s and 1980s.

The purpose and meaning of verification was easy enough to identify; the problems arose when it came to defining the degree of certainty required and the centrality of verification mechanisms in determining compliance with treaties. Some felt that compliance would be more likely that not and that verification was a question of insurance rather than necessity. Schelling and Halperin, for example, felt that 'inspection has been overemphasized in most discussions of arms control',[60] and that apparent treaty breaches 'will usually be a matter of intent, rather than simply a matter of action'.[61] Similarly Robert Bowie argued that 'inspection should be viewed as a technique for reinforcing and maintaining the self-interest of the parties in the continued effective operation of the system.'[62]

Not everyone was so sanguine. Fred Iklé felt that compliance was perhaps *the* crucial issue in arms control and that effective verification was essential for ensuring compliance. Moreover, he felt that signatories must always be prepared to break off an agreement to punish the adversary if the other side was discovered to be cheating. Violations could only be deterred if the adversary knew that detected cheating would lead to an acceleration in military competition.[63]

For Bowie compliance questions had to take account not just of the existence of an alleged breach, but also the scale of the transgression and its possible implications. Verification had to deal with detection and possible compensatory countermeasures before facing the central issue, which was how likely was evasion and how did the risk of non-compliance compare with the risks involved in not having an agreement at all?[64] Some risk would clearly have to be endured since there could never be absolute certainty in such a subjective area of policy. Getting the facts would always be the most straightforward part of the verification process; the harder part would involve 'arguing over the interpretations, projections, forecasts and evaluations of significance of the facts at hand'.[65]

Verification was deemed a matter of greater concern to the US than the Soviet Union simply because the former was an open society and the latter was not. This would doubtless mean that in bargaining sequences the Soviet Union would tend to see agreement on monitoring procedures as representing a Soviet concession since they deemed their military secrecy to be a considerable strategic asset.[66]

Since the Soviet Union would deem the verification procedures a concession, while the US would see them as representing a calculated risk, initial agreements were likely to be those which involved a minimum requirement for verification, or in which this could be done by non-intrusive means. Even so, in these early agreements 'the degree of intensity of inspection is most likely to seem out of proportion to the modest initial restrictions or reductions.'[67] These were prophetic words.

Conclusion

What stands out from the early writings on arms control is just how well they have stood the test of time. Bearing this in mind, Hedley Bull's comments on the ultimate purpose of arms control were ominous given the degree of hope with which the public would come to regard arms control over the following quarter of a century. Writing of the technical problems standing in the way of arms control he declared that

> The view that international negotiations about arms control are concerned with the search for solutions to these problems, or that their failure to issue in agreements arises from the difficulty of finding these solutions, is on the whole, mistaken. For the protracted public conversation of the powers about arms control should be viewed not as a cooperative attempt to solve a problem, but as a theme in their political relations.[68]

2

The Development of Arms Control

Arms control has developed the same kind of mindless momentum
associated with other large-scale bureaucratic enterprises.
Burt, 'International Security and the Relevance of Arms Control'[1]

Introduction

The arms control approach has been firmly in place since 1962, the
year in which the extraordinary outburst of 'golden age' arms control
writing came to an end, and in which the trauma of the Cuban
Missile Crisis set the superpowers on the path towards greater accommodation of each other's security needs in an attempt to avoid a
nuclear catastrophe. At the end of that crisis President John
F. Kennedy wrote to the Soviet Premier, Nikita Khrushchev, 'I
agree with you that we must devote urgent attention to the problem of
disarmament, as it relates to the whole world and also to critical
areas. Perhaps now as we step back from danger, we can together
make real progress in this vital field.'[2] The following year in his
historic speech at American University Kennedy summed up the
ultimate rationale of the arms control approach with the hope that 'if
we cannot now end our differences, at least we can help make the
world safe for diversity.'[3] As a senator from Massachusetts and a
former congressman from a seat which included Harvard, it is
perhaps not surprising that he was receptive to the arms control ideal.
As a senator he had advocated many of the approaches suggested by
the arms controllers.[4] An interesting feature of his brief presidency
was the breakthrough in arms control achieved in 1963 which, while

representing the onset of the 'era of negotiations
the inherent limitations of the arms control appr

One of the lessons thrown up by the Cuban M
inadequacy of existing facilities for rapid commu
superpower leaderships. Khrushchev and Kenn
to establish a direct telex link between the Kreml
This so-called 'hot-line' was operational by the su
same summer Kennedy's direct involvement led
sion of the Limited Test Ban Treaty (LTBT) with Britain and the
Soviet Union. This agreement banned the conducting of nuclear tests
in the atmosphere, under water or in space. Kennedy felt that the
treaty represented the greatest achievement of his presidency; yet it
was also a disappointment, since his own preference had been for a
comprehensive test ban (CTB) to end nuclear testing completely.
The outcome of the LTBT set a number of precedents for arms
control. Subsequent agreements also tended to be partial: for
example, in 1972 a Biological Weapons Convention was signed by
the superpowers. This treaty banned biological weapons and ordered
the destruction of existing stockpiles. It therefore represented the only
example of true total disarmament of a weapon category to have
occurred since 1945. Initially, however, it had formed part of
negotiations to ban both chemical and biological weapons, the former
being infinitely more significant. The 1972 convention, while useful,
thus represented a retreat from the more difficult, but more
important, objective of a chemical weapons treaty.

The nuclear testing issue itself was back on the agenda by the
1970's, and once again partial rather than comprehensive restraints
were negotiated. In 1974 the Threshold Test Ban Treaty (TTBT) was
signed, whereby the US and the Soviet Union agreed not to carry out
any nuclear tests with an explosive yield of more than 150 kilotons.
The treaty was significant in that it raised doubts about some of the
arguments made against a CTB. Opponents argued that continued
testing was required in order to refine existing warheads and to
sample the stockpile for reliability. Yet both sides continued (and
continue) to deploy warheads in excess of 150 kilotons: for example,
the 350 kiloton warheads on Minuteman 3 and Peacekeeper, and the
Soviet ICBM force, whose warheads range from the 550 kiloton
SS-19 to the 3.6 megaton warheads on some of the SS-17 force. No
loss of confidence seems to have occurred as a result of the treaty.

eless, neither this treaty nor the 1976 treaty extending the
limitations to 'peaceful' nuclear explosions paved the way to the
pid conclusion of a CTB, which is as far away as ever.

These partial treaties raise the question of to what extent should the
best be the enemy of the good? Measured against the effects of a
comprehensive test ban the treaties of 1963, 1974 and 1976 can be
seen as political palliatives, mere cosmetic agreements. President
Carter in 1977 called the TTBT and the PNET 'a wholly inadequate
step' and refused to ask the Senate for ratification, preferring to seek a
comprehensive ban instead. In the event he was no more successful in
achieving a comprehensive treaty than President Kennedy had been
and it was not until 1987 that the two threshold treaties were finally
sent to the Senate. This was unfortunate because the treaties contained verification clauses, particularly relating to on-site inspection
(OSI) and test-site geological data exchanges, which were not only
significant Soviet concessions in themselves but would have provided
the confidence and data to make more restrictive treaties far easier to
achieve subsequently. President Carter would have been better
advised to have taken the two birds in the hand before going after the
one in the bush.

Agreements and Negotiations

Between 1963 and 1987 negotiations took place on a wide range of
arms control issues, leading in many cases to agreement, particularly
in the first half of the 1970s. In retrospect, however, doubt has been
cast on the value of the exercise and so it is worth looking at the
negotiations and the treaties that did, or did not, emerge from them.

The LTBTs have already been mentioned. One class of agreements
was even more limited in impact, and these were the non-armament
agreements. Four treaties come into this broad category: the 1959
Antarctic Treaty, the Outer Space Treaty and Tlatelolco Treaty (both
1967), and the 1971 Seabed Treaty. The 1979 Moon Treaty would
also be relevant, but neither superpower shows any sign of acceding
to it. All these treaties have in common an attempt to prevent military
competition from being introduced into an area that had hitherto
been free of such activity.

The Antarctic Treaty set the precedent for those that followed. It
prohibited the establishment of military bases or the use of Antarctica

for the holding of military manoeuvres or the testing of weapons. The Soviet Union agreed to periodic on-site inspection of its Antarctic bases. Obviously the treaty did not in any sense mark a major military concession by the superpowers since there were no reasons why they would wish to use Antarctica for any of the proscribed activities. However, this might not always be the case and it therefore seemed valuable to prohibit certain courses of action before the states became committed to them. The Treaty of Tlatelolco (a suburb of Mexico City where the treaty was negotiated) established a Latin American nuclear-free zone. The Outer Space Treaty was similar to the Antarctic Treaty, banning the testing or deployment of 'weapons of mass destruction' in earth's orbit or on other bodies in the solar system and forbidding military manoeuvres on the moon. Finally came the Seabed Treaty which banned the placing of weapons of mass destruction on or below the seabed.

The criticism made of these treaties is that they are meaningless. In the case of the Antarctic and Seabed treaties there was no reason to believe such activities would ever be contemplated; indeed, the seabed treaty has been compared to a treaty forbidding states to bolt their aircraft to runways. In the case of the Tlatelolco Treaty the main problem is that the most likely nuclear-weapon candidates, Argentina and Brazil, have not become full parties to the treaty. However, it can be argued that the treaty's real value would be seen if strategic or technological developments made the areas in question genuinely attractive to the superpowers.

The evidence of the Outer Space Treaty is not encouraging in this regard. When it was signed it was assumed that it had closed off space as an area into which weaponry could be introduced. Nevertheless, within a year of its signature the Soviet Union began testing a co-orbital anti-satellite (ASAT) weapon in space, a programme that was continued intermittently throughout the following decade. A US ASAT programme was initiated under President Carter and flight-testing began under his successor. Moreover, under President Reagan, the SDI programme was begun, which envisaged emplacing a vast array of weaponry in space, potentially including the nuclear-induced 'Excalibur' X-ray laser. While it could be argued that neither of the superpower ASATs used 'weapons of mass destruction' and were therefore not strictly-speaking illegal under the 1967 treaty, it is patently obvious that they violated the spirit of the treaty and thwarted the intentions of its framers. Furthermore, the ASAT programmes and SDI implied that once the superpowers found valid military reasons to enter the areas covered by the non-armament treaties they would be able to come up with 'reinterpretations' which would enable them to do whatever they wished. If this is indeed the case then the treaties are clearly not worth the paper they are written on.

The 1963 Hot-Line agreement also set a precedent. The early arms control theorists had stressed the importance of clear and rapid communication between the superpowers, and the 1963 treaty was the first attempt to implement this advice. Others followed, designed to improve the ability to communicate directly during crises and to reduce the danger of nuclear war breaking out through misunderstanding or accident. The 1963 treaty set up a duplex wire-telegraph and this was updated in 1971 to establish a system based on two satellite communication circuits. This became fully operational in 1978. In 1984 a further refinement was added, allowing pictures as well as text to be transmitted.

The influence of the arms controllers was also clearly visible in the 1971 US–Soviet agreement on 'Measures to Reduce the Risk of Outbreak of Nuclear War'. This provided for unilateral improvements to each side's 'fail-safe' devices and techniques, immediate notification of the other party in the event of an accidental or unauthorized incident involving possible detonation of a nuclear weapon, immediate notification of missile warning alerts and advance notification of planned test missile launches. Of less obvious value was the 1973 Agreement on the Prevention of Nuclear War which called for 'urgent consultations' in the event that there seemed to be a risk of imminent nuclear war between the two countries, or between one of them and a third nuclear-armed country.

One other agreement signed at this time also derived from a central concern of the arms controllers. This was the 1968 Non-Proliferation Treaty, NPT. Concerns about nuclear proliferation featured prominently in all the books which form the core of the 'golden age' arms control literature. The NPT was a complex multilateral negotiation; however, one aspect of the 1968 treaty is highly relevant to the subject of superpower arms control. Although well over a hundred states are signatories, the NPT is essentially a treaty between two parties; the nuclear weapon states on one side and the non-nuclear states on the other. The non-nuclear states promised not to try to acquire nuclear weapons in return for two things: access to peaceful nuclear energy and a genuine effort by the nuclear weapon states to divest themselves of those weapons. Article VI of the NPT calls upon the nuclear powers to 'pursue negotiations in good faith on effective measures relating to cessation of the nuclear arms race at an early date and to nuclear disarmament'. The audit of superpower success or failure in this field is therefore clearly of relevance to the future of the NPT as a barrier to nuclear proliferation.

The primary evidence of superpower effort to live up to Article VI of the NPT were the SALT treaties of 1972 and 1979. These agreements will be mentioned *ad nauseam* throughout this book so only an outline of their terms is given here. SALT I came in two parts, an ABM treaty limiting each side to only two ABM sites (reduced by agreement to one each in 1974) and an 'interim' offensive arms agreement. The latter essentially set an upper limit to the arms build-up then under way, specifying, for example, that no additional ICBM launchers could be added to those operational on 1 July 1972, that SLBMs would be limited to those operational in May 1972, that no new 'heavy' ICBMs could be deployed, that future modernization and replacement could only be on a one-for-one basis and that the US would be allowed 44 submarines carrying 710 SLBMs and the USSR 62 submarines carrying 740 SLBMs. As its title implied the treaty was seen only as setting ceilings not to be breached while a definitive SALT II treaty was negotiated.

A lot of hopes were therefore riding on the SALT II negotiations, which were asked to carry a tremendous burden in terms of the implications for future superpower relations. Once again President Carter was unwise not to move to a quick conclusion of the draft SALT II treaty the Ford administration had produced before it left office. Had he done so he could have moved on to his preferred deeper cuts in SALT III where the Soviet Union was planning to offer 10 per cent reductions as its opening bid. Accepting that would have meant that in two successive agreements the Soviet Union would have reduced its strategic forces by 20 per cent leaving arms control with a far more positive public image. As it was, by time the treaty was signed in June 1979 it was being overtaken by events. The treaty hearings which did take place before Carter asked the Senate to suspend its consideration demonstrated that there were no major flaws in the treaty itself; certainly no 'fatal' ones.

SALT II established a limit of 2,400 strategic missiles and bombers for each side. Sub-ceilings limited each side to 1,320 weapons equipped with MIRV warheads or air-launched cruise missiles. No more than 1,200 ballistic missiles could carry MIRVed warheads and ICBMs would have a limit of ten warheads per missile, SLBMs a limit of 14. Each side could deploy only one new ICBM before December 1985. At the time it was signed critics argued that some of its clauses created dangerous precedents for SALT III. In the event there was to be no SALT III; by 1980 the SALT-style arms control process had ground to a halt, with the arms control community in confusion as to what had gone wrong.

Meaning and Purpose

As the 1960s progressed towards the 1970s the meaning of arms control evolved steadily away from the ideas of its original proponents and acquired an essentially political rather than strategic purpose, or at least strategic stability was relegated to the position of being simply one of the many objectives arms control was called upon to advance.

The most notable new objective, which clearly sprang from political rather than strategic considerations, was the pursuit of reductions as a primary objective. As noted in chapter 1, the original proponents of arms control did not see steady reductions as a major objective. They were not opposed to reductions, they just did not think they were either necessary or important. Moreover, they believed that there was a crucial minimum beyond which no process of reduction should be allowed to go.[5]

When superpower parity and the strategic stability that went with it finally arrived, however, it was at very high force levels. For various reasons, these levels were far higher even than those called for by 'assured destruction' requirements. The awareness that even on the most pessimistic assumptions both sides possessed an enormous degree of redundancy or 'overkill', coupled with the seemingly endless upwards spiral of warhead totals, led to a general political environment favourable to reductions. This feeling was widespread among the public, which believed instinctively that the fewer nuclear weapons on each side the better. It was also held by mainstream arms controllers such as Johan Holst.[6] It was most vigorously propounded by the 'fellow-travellers' of the arms control approach, the intellectual disarmers who supported arms control as the pursuit of regular partial disarmament. This outlook meant that any agreement which failed to produce numerical reductions, irrespective of whether or not it attained the original aims of arms control, would be deemed a failure. Judged in this light it was argued that 'arms control has not served well the cause of disarmament.'[7] In fact, of course, it was never supposed to serve the cause of disarmament at all and only gradually gained such a goal as a result of political pressures from without and the efforts of the disarmers to redefine its purpose from within.

The arms control community at its inception was a broad church. At its core were the strategic analysts, dedicated to achieving a stable balance of power. Politically it won support from conservatives who saw it as preferable to the disarmament approach which had dominated prior to the late 1950s, and it won radical support by seeming to hold out hope of some restraint in arms build-up. As the 1960s unfolded and the 'danger' of disarmament faded from view, conservative support for arms control faded as well. At the same time radicals became disillusioned as the approach failed to produce the hoped-for reductions. The arms control constituency therefore began to shrink, a shrinkage which could only be halted by morale-boosting achievements.

Such achievements proved desperately hard to achieve. During the 1960s the US adopted the logical policy that once the capacity to inflict a certain level of damage on the Soviet Union had been achieved there was no need to acquire further nuclear weapons. To allow for misfires, malfunctions, inaccuracy and the general effect of what Clausewitz called 'friction' in war, a certain number of weapons over and above the theoretical minimum would need to be maintained. However, the US also adopted the triad approach in which its nuclear weapons would be carried on manned bombers and on ground and submarine launched ballistic missiles. The triad was an insurance policy. At any one time the Soviets might develop highly effective defences against bombers or improve their anti-submarine warfare capability, but if any 'leg' of the triad was threatened in this way the other two could carry the burden of deterrence. Even if two legs were threatened simultaneously the third would still be capable of deterring. This approach meant that *each* leg of the triad must be capable of inflicting unacceptable levels of destruction on the Soviet Union on its own. The triad concept, together with 'assured destruction', worst-case assumptions and generous margins of error, meant that the US acquired an enormous degree of overkill. It was to this very high level that the Soviet Union was allowed to catch up and achieve parity in the early 1970s.

The public unease seems to have arisen not so much from the absolute levels of weaponry, but from the perception of an endlessly increasing total. A crucial failure of SALT I therefore was to miss the opportunity to ban multiple warhead missiles, MIRVs. Had SALT I truly 'capped' the arms race at 1972 levels it would have been perceived as a profound achievement. By allowing MIRVing to proceed unchecked, however, this opportunity was missed. Launcher totals remained stable, but warhead totals increased dramatically, fuelling public perceptions of an arms race that had not been brought under control.

SALT I was a critical missed opportunity for arms control. Its two component parts, the ABM Treaty and the Interim Agreement on Offensive Arms, marked a simultaneous high and low point of achievement for the arms control approach as it had evolved to that point, and the differing degrees of achievement contained the seeds of self-destruction. The ABM Treaty was clearly a major arms control success. By locking the superpowers into a position of mutual vulnerability it reinforced a deterrence relationship of marked stability. A MIRV ban would have massively reinforced this. By allowing MIRVing to go ahead, however, the superpowers created a situation in which each side's retaliatory forces would become threatened by a 'weapon-rich' adversary with more nuclear warheads than there were counterforce targets to aim at. ICBM vulnerability flowed inexorably from MIRV. As each side became increasingly aware of the vulnerability of its retaliatory forces, so each would look for ways to protect its ICBMs. In doing so each would initiate steps, most dramatically President Reagan's SDI, which would undermine the purpose of the ABM Treaty.

In this sense SALT I *was* 'fatally flawed', more so than its successor. It did not plesae conservatives, who wanted no constraints at all; it failed to satisfy liberals who noted the likely increase in warheads; and ultimately it failed to satisfy the arms controllers, who rejoiced in the ABM Treaty but were only too aware of the problems lying in ambush for the two agreements.

The inherent difficulties in producing meaningful superpower arms control accords are looked at in subsequent chapters. A few further points are worth making about SALT I here. For all its flaws, it did represent an enormous breakthrough. For the first time the superpowers had signed a bilateral agreement limiting their ability to acquire additional weapons for use against each other. They did this at a time of great pressure. It is commonplace nowadays for commentators to look back on the early 1970s as an era of cosy *détente* and goodwill between the superpowers. This is a myth. SALT I was negotiated and signed against the background of the American war in Vietnam, the Soviet invasion of Czechoslovakia, Soviet fears of an emerging Sino–American rapprochement at a time when Soviet and Chinese forces were fighting a 'hot' war over a disputed border, growing tensions over the Middle East and a series of spy scandals. Relations, in other words, were anything but cordial. Just before SALT I was signed US bombers caused Russian casualties in a raid on shipping in Haiphong harbour. In the circumstances SALT I was, and remains, a remarkable diplomatic achievement.

Its very success created a precedent, however. It tended to tie arms control into the strait-jacket of large-scale formal negotiations. Whereas the original proponents of arms control had stressed flexibility of approach, tacit as well as explicit agreements, small or short-term as well as omnibus treaties, the SALT I agreements set a pattern for SALT II and subsequent negotiations. Moreover the early advocates had been at pains to stress that there were limits to what arms control could achieve. President Nixon and his successors felt obliged for political reasons dramatically to overstate the likely effects of the treaties they negotiated and to promise that any deficiencies would be put right in the subsequent agreements which were anticipated. It was increasingly difficult for subsequent treaties to meet these expectations. Oversold for domestic political reasons, the process was steadily brought into disrepute. The public, geared to expect too much from the process, tended to interpret 'success' as meaning reductions. By the 1980s newspaper writers were having to remind the public that this had never been the central objective of arms control and to reflect that 'people not versed in the arcane literature of arms control are usually surprised to learn that main-stream specialists have never placed much emphasis on arms reductions.'[8] But after SALT I even the arms controllers were having to admit that the public had acquired a perception of the objectives of arms control which centred on limitation and reduction of weaponry and which assumed that this could only be done through explicit international agreement.[9]

The inability to deliver these major reductions even in SALT II led to an increasing public awareness of an arms control objective that was always implicit in the approach from its inception. The pursuit of arms control by governments which used the rhetoric of disarmament, confident in the knowledge that the complexities of the bargaining process would rule out any radical action, revealed arms control as a mechanism for legitimizing the arms race. Arms control efforts demonstrated that 'necessary force modernisation was taking place within a framework of at least a serious attempt at restraint and cooperation.'[10] For the strategic community there was nothing sinister about this; they preferred stability at lower levels of armament if possible, but they saw military power and the nuclear condition as facts of life which could not, and should not, be wished away. For them the relationship of arms control to the arms race was the need to manage that which could not be abolished; in John Garnett's words: 'for the disarmers it is a philosophy of despair; for the arms controllers it is all there is.'[11]

Methods

The experience with arms control during the 1960s and 1970s produced a major debate over the methods most likely to produce success. From a position of remarkable consensus in the early 1970s the arms control community began to fragment on the issue of methodology by the end of the decade.

One disagreement has already been mentioned: namely, the argument over how important visible reductions were to the process. There was no doubt about their political salience and for some it was the obvious route to take. It produced a major critique, however, by Thomas Schelling (one of the founding fathers of arms control), who argued that the shift from concern about the *character* of weapons to concern about their *numbers* was the crucial difference between arms control negotiations before and after 1971.[12] Indeed Schelling claimed that arms control was being pursued without reference to its original guiding philosophy and that reductions in numbers only really mattered if the ultimate goal was zero,' but hardly anyone who takes arms control seriously believes that zero is the goal.'[13]

The implications of this difference are profound. Arms control as pursued during the 1970s tended to concentrate upon negotiability. Weapon systems were divided up for bargaining purposes into manageable categories such as ground and air-launched cruise missiles, or strategic and intermediate-range ballistic missiles. These categories did not necessarily distinguish between the *capabilities* that arms control was designed to inhibit, such as first-strike capacity or vulnerability to attack. Thus, for example, Schelling noted that submarine-launched cruise missiles (SLCMs) were frowned upon by the arms control community because they were hard to count and therefore difficult to verify. Because verifiability was a *sine qua non* of agreement they could not be limited and seemed therefore a threatening development. Yet this flies in the face of early arms control thinking. SLCMs are too slow to be a first-strike weapon, difficult to defend against, impossible to locate on station and cheap to produce: in arms control terms an ideal weapon which need not be subject to constraint anyway since it could neither pre-empt itself nor be the subject of a successful pre-emptive strike by the adversary.[14]

There is no doubt that in intellectual terms Schelling is absolutely right. However, politically this position is no longer a realistic option. The manner in which arms control has been conducted for the past 20 years and the way in which politicians have geared the public to expect arms control to freeze or reduce numbers means that a central original tenet of the arms control approach has effectively been buried.

This is not an isolated example. Early writers on arms control were by no means hostile to the idea of unilateral initiatives as a way forward. This is no longer the case. The track record of attempts in this area is deemed to be too discouraging to warrant any optimism. In 1961 the Soviet Union resumed nuclear testing despite US restraint in this field. Conversely in 1985–6 the US continued to carry out nuclear tests despite a self-imposed Soviet moratorium. Soviet

ASAT tests were carried out in the 1970s although no comparable US system existed, and neither did the Soviet Union follow the other sides lead in deactivating its permitted ABM site in 1976. The US' long-range bomber force was not reduced when the expected Soviet strategic bomber build-up failed to materialize in the 1960s. The problem is partly that the force structures of the two sides are asymmetrical. Each side has acquired weapons to suit its own military doctrine. It is therefore not self-evident that restraint by one side will automatically produce restraint by the other. Moreover, the basic mistrust which lies at the heart of international politics is not inevitably diminished by unilateral gestures, since arms are a reflection rather than a cause of tension.[15] This is not to say that arms build-ups do not add to tension, or that reductions cannot improve the climate somewhat, but they are a very long way from being a panacea. States are heavily inclined towards caution in security matters, as NATO's suspicious reaction to the barrage of Soviet arms control offers in 1985-7 demonstrated. The basic rule of thumb is that 'the consequences of mistaking enemies for friends are much more dangerous than the consequences of regarding friends as enemies.'[16]

Instead of pursuing the various approaches advocated by the early arms controllers, political leaders became obsessed by the pursuit of comprehensive accords. Whereas the Partial Test Ban Treaty took only weeks to negotiate, SALT I took four years and SALT II took seven. Apart from being a diplomatically wearing exercise, such extended negotiations mean that by the time a treaty is concluded it may no longer be relevant to the concerns which inspired it.[17]

Dissatisfaction with the ponderous nature of the SALT process led many arms controllers to advocate smaller, more frequent agreements as the best way forward.' Small steps or large steps for a short duration'[18] would, it was felt, unblock the logjam and create a momentum of progress. This argument is persuasive, though there is a counterargument. Given that even the epic negotiations like SALT produced such limited outcomes it may be, as Kruzel has suggested, that only by seeking very ambitious goals can arms control produce even modest results,[19] and that attempts to pursue modest goals would produce only cosmetic agreements.

Concern with the need to sustain 'momentum' was a feature of arms control thinking after 1972. Arms control was seen as a process which needed to be nourished by regular achievements. Regular Soviet–US summit meetings were advocated as one way of achieving this since they would force the superpower leaderships to focus on the arms control issues and give the necessary political impetus to the negotiating teams.[20]

On the whole, however, the disappointment of the 1970s did not lead to any renaissance in arms control thinking; on the contrary, the paucity of new ideas is striking. One exception, 'in a field where new ideas are rare',[21] was the suggestion by Christoph Bertram that the obsession with numerical parity be dropped in favour of an approach which concentrated upon the military missions weapons systems were designed to implement. The focus would not be on 'who had what?' but upon 'who could do what?', a much more productive line of military inquiry. Equality of options rather than numbers would be the objective.[22]

The arms control approach from 1963 to 1979, while disappointing as far as the nature of the agreements signed, did at least create the foundations on which future success could be built. A whole new terminology was created to which both sides could relate; basic principles for negotiation were agreed upon, and mechanisms for counting weapons systems were developed. Agreement was reached on what types of verification techniques were required and how much deliberate deception was tolerable. Data exchanges, unprecedented in Russian history, were begun. New mechanisms for resolving disputes, such as the Standing Consultative Commission for the SALT treaties, were established. These were all permanent gains which created an infrastructure into which subsequent negotiations could be fitted with comparative ease.

Problems of Arms Control

During the 1970s the benefits of arms control were oversold by US leaders. Inevitably this produced public disillusionment when the meagre results were compared to the grandiose rhetoric. The early proponents of arms control were certainly not to blame for this development. Virtually all of them had been at pains to emphasize the limitations of the approach and their hopes for it were modest. These hopes did not include either ending the nuclear competition or transforming the superpower relationship into a security community. President Kennedy stressed this at the time of the 1963 Partial Test Ban Treaty.

Evidence from opinion polls seems to indicate that the US public were more sophisticated than their leaders on this issue during the 1970s. It has been argued that US policy-makers failed to educate the American people as to what *détente* meant. Whereas the Soviet Union stressed that 'detente is not a barrier to social transformation' and that the worldwide struggle against capitalism would continue, US politicians chose to ignore the Soviet interpretation of arms control as a limited strategic arrangement and to make claims for arms control which it simply could not deliver. This misconception was worsened by Congress's actions in linking future progress in arms control to favourable developments in Soviet domestic as well as foreign policy.[23]

Yet it is not at all clear that the American public accepted this picture as uncritically as is often assumed. A month after SALT I was signed a Harris poll for the Washington Post revealed that 65 per cent of the public believed that 'the Cold War had not ended.'[24] During the 1970s as a whole polls consistently showed that US public opinion did not think that arms control agreements with the Soviet Union meant that the need for military strength had declined or that competition with the Soviet Union would significantly diminish. SALT I was signed in 1972, a protocol reducing the number of permitted ABM sites to one each and a TTBT were signed in 1974 and in 1976 a PNET was concluded. Yet in each of these years there was a steady increase in the number of Americans worried by Soviet foreign policy activities, the percentages 'concerned' rising from 24 per cent in 1972 to 37 per cent in 1974 and 50 per cent in 1976. In the same period the numbers not very worried by Soviet actions fell from 27 per cent to 18 per cent.[25] At the time of SALT II in 1979 opinion polls indicated that the American public wanted a new strategic arms control agreement with the Soviet Union (81 per cent in favour) but did not expect this to enable the US to reduce its defence spending, only 16 per cent favouring such a reduction.[26]

These figures appear to indicate that the American public did not see arms control through rose-tinted glasses. They also indicate that the arms control process did not of itself lead to an improvement in perceptions of the adversary. A number of elements may have contributed to this. The 'overselling' of *détente* and arms control was no doubt one factor, producing an obvious discrepancy between what the government alleged could be expected from the agreements and what in fact actually happened. The arms control agreements only placed a limited number of constraints on each side and the continuing (legal) build-up in unconstrained areas undoubtedly disappointed a public led to believe that a 'cap' had been put on the arms race. In practice the superpower governments felt that they were moving as fast as they could on the issue. Since they believed that they were at the *beginning* of an arms control process, it was hardly surprising that neither side interfered seriously with its long-term programmes at that stage and both sides felt obliged to hedge against the possibility of a breakdown in the process.

The actual process itself also had an unexpectedly alarming impact upon the general population. The negotiations led to increased media attention on the relative size and capabilities of the superpower arsenals and tended to focus attention on the force disparities, irrespective of their operational significance. This was all the more significant since it was a period of great technological advance in which the two sides were bargaining over weapon systems of uncertain performance. Since there had never been a full-scale nuclear war it was not at all clear which systems would actually be the most effective and therefore decisions on what to retain and, what to reduce would always be open to attack whichever way they went. The pursuit of parity led to the feeling that equality in all systems must be attained irrespective of whether one side actually needed those systems. Senator Jackson's criticisms of the Soviet 'heavy' missile monopoly in SALT I were a case in point. The US did not have such missiles in its inventory because it did not need them, yet for many the SS-18 monopoly became a potent symbol of Soviet advantage.

The diplomatic costs of entering into arms control negotiations emerged only slowly. For many, negotiations were an inherently good thing, irrespective of outcome. Nations, it was felt, should attempt to improve their relationships and be seen trying to do so. But there are risks involved in entering into negotiations. If the talks break down in failure with each side blaming the other for the breakdown, then the relationship may end up worse than it was before the talks began. The negotiations on intermediate-range nuclear forces (INF) of 1982–3 led only to rancour and a Soviet walkout.

Disillusionment with arms control also developed because the negotiations in the 1980s began to resemble the sterile disarmament talks of the 1950s. Arms control in the 1960s was based on the assumption that negotiations would be serious and agreements would be sought which were modest, cautious and above all negotiable: that is, there was good reason to think the deal would be acceptable to both sides after the usual haggling over details. Deals would be designed to stabilize an emerging strategic balance and bring limited but significant increases in the security of each side. However, negotiations can be used to pursue propaganda goals, as they were during the 1950s, and during the 1980s this approach re-emerged as the primary, if not the only, impetus behind the superpower proposals. The acceptance of the need to see the other side's fears and rights was abandoned in favour of a return to the outright pursuit of comparative advantage and the use of negotiations as a propaganda platform. Not surprisingly criticism of the whole arms control approach mounted steadily.

Criticisms of Arms Control

By 1979 it was possible for one observer to state confidently that 'the past enthusiasm for arms control has waned considerably. Arms control is indeed, in crisis.'[27] This view was echoed by many others, both theorists and practitioners. Arms control, at least as it had been pursued for the previous 25 years, was seen to have come to the end of the road.[28]

Some of the attacks on arms control derived from a basic hostility towards the whole concept and were simply self-serving. For example, Eugene Rostow and others argued that arms control lulled Americans into a false sense of security hostile to necessary defence spending.[29] As already noted there is really no evidence to support this view; indeed, the obsession with numerical parity in all areas and the requirement for 'bargaining chips' tended to have the opposite effect.

Other criticisms were more painful because they came, as it were, from the body of the kirk. By the early 1980s, although arms control had brought benefits, these were rather 'underwhelming' given the enormous commitment of human energy over a quarter of a century that had gone into producing them. It seemed increasingly that arms control 'had become an end in itself, pursued with great energy but without much sense of purpose or direction.'[30] Some, such as Schelling, went further, claiming that the doctrine itself had been lost sight of.[31]

Criticism was not limited to the practice of arms control but extended also to its original formulation. There was a sense that arms control theory was by no means as internally consistent as it had originally seemed. The original objectives, to reduce the risk of war, its destructiveness if it occurred and the costs of being prepared for it, were not always mutually compatible: 'No one knew precisely how to reduce the risk of a type of war that had never been fought; most people intuitively sensed that reducing damage might actually increase the risk of nuclear conflict. Any sensible strategic analyst would have been happy to increase defence spending if doing so would purchase a diminished risk of war.'[32]

This was true and indeed many of the assumptions which underlay the early arms control approach suffered both from inconsistencies and from the failure to realize that the major negotiating partner might bring a quite different set of assumptions to the bargaining table. There was an implicit belief on the US side during the 1960s that their strategic doctrine was so obviously superior that once the more backward Russians grasped it, a dialogue could ensue which would make negotiations comparatively straightforward. In practice Soviet strategic thought proved equally sophisticated but different in approach and the intellectual borrowing which occurred in the 1970s turned out to be a two-way street. Neither were either side's views immutable. The US spent the early part of the 1970s convincing the Soviet Union that strategic defences were a bad thing which should be severely constrained. By the early 1980s, having reversed its position, the US was attempting with difficulty to convince Moscow that the Soviet position in 1970 had in fact been correct all along and that strategic defences should be encouraged.

The advent of the New Right into government with President Reagan in 1981 brought into office an administration deeply suspicious of arms control. Even the so-called moderates, such as Richard Burt, were scarcely less hostile to arms control than hawks such as Richard Perle. Burt had described as a 'fallacy' the idea that the purpose of arms control negotiations was to reduce military instability.[33] Even the idea that arms competition should be limited by negotiation was attacked.[34]

Many of the criticisms made in the early 1980s represented an overreaction against the limited successes of the 1970s. Arms control was being condemned by contrasting it to a preferred ideal situation of even better agreements rather than with the more likely alternative of no arms control agreements at all. By the mid-1980s the 'failures' of the 1970s were looking a lot better in comparison to the seven-year arms control vacuum that followed. To some extent traditional US impatience was to blame for the scepticism in that country. The slow pace of achievement led not to a revision of expectations and a steady attempt to overcome obstacles, but rather to a root and branch questioning of the very nature and purpose of the exercise. This was not unhealthy; after 20 years an effort to review and rethink basic premises was clearly overdue, but the timing was unfortunate. By 1980 too few in the US were speaking up for arms control. Proponents were criticizing the paucity of achievement and casting doubt on the methods being pursued, while critics were effectively seeking the abandonment of the whole exercise. At a time when a sea-change in US politics was occurring arms control found itself friendless, without a powerful constituency to sustain it in adversity. Half a decade would be lost before the real virtues of arms control became widely appreciated once more, for while 'critics found the achievements of SALT II wanting . . . every year that passed without a better agreement was a reminder of reductions that were declined from an already negotiated baseline.'[35] Yet with every year that went by arms control suffered a loss of its greatest asset, the sense that it was realistic and feasible.

The question, therefore, is why did arms control prove to be such a toothless tiger after 1960? As noted in chapter 1, the early proponents of arms control were in fact well aware of the obstacles it was likely to face. In practice, however, those obstacles proved even more daunting than they had anticipated and a number of these will now be examined to determine their impact upon the success or failure of arms control in the last quarter of a century.

3

Arms Control and Technological Change

The pace of technology is outstripping man's ingenuity to find ways of
placing political restraints upon it.

Pierre, 'The Diplomacy of SALT'[1]

Introduction

In his Farewell Address to the American people, President Eisenhower
warned them to be on guard against certain insidious dangers. His
reference to the 'military–industrial complex' is frequently quoted.
Less well known is another section of the same speech in which he
warned of the danger 'that public policy could itself become the
captive of a scientific–technological elite'. Eisenhower was referring
in particular to the potential dangers posed by a technological arms
race, in which the essential political realities would be determined by
the activities of the scientists working in the weapons laboratories
rather than their political masters. In a lecture published in 1980
Lord Zuckerman argued that effectively Eisenhower's prediction had
become reality, that the nuclear weapon scientists 'have succeeded in
creating a world with an irrational foundation, on which a new set of
political realities has had in turn to be built. They have become the
alchemists of our times, working in secret ways which cannot be
divulged, casting spells which embrace us all'.[2]

The question of whether or not technology drives the arms race is
crucial to any assessment of the limitations and possibilities of the
arms control process. If the arms race is a function of inevitable

advances in military technology then the attempt to control it through political agreements may be foredoomed to failure. Even the perception that this is so among leading politicians might cause it to become a self-fulfilling prophecy.[3] Against this, the generally held picture of statesmen basing their foreign and defence policies upon rational assessments of need and opportunity would see a technology-driven arms race as too deterministic an explanation for the difficulties of arms control.[4] It is therefore necessary to examine the context in which weapons procurement takes place, the forces guiding acquisition decisions and the nature of the weapons development process in the US and the Soviet Union, with a view to determining whether the technology is out of control and what the potential impact of arms control is in this area.

Threat Perception

States acquire weapons for a wide variety of reasons, many of them related to their foreign policy objectives.[5] One factor invariably present, however, is the perception of being threatened by one or more actors in the international system. The greater the threat perceived, the stronger is the desire to acquire greater military power in order to deter aggression against oneself. Threat perception is a function of a potential adversary's capabilities and intentions. Quite often a negative attitude towards an adversary's intentions will produce assumptions about that adversary's actual or desired capabilities. It is assumed that if the adversary is *capable* of producing a certain weapon system then it *will* produce that weapon system, and produce it in large numbers.

It is never possible to be absolutely sure what the other side are working on because weapons developments are shrouded in secrecy. Given that it might take 10–15 years to develop a countermeasure to anything the adversary deploys, the most prudent policy is to gear research towards anticipating future threats and military requirements and then developing the appropriate technology. Thus Defense Secretary McNamara justified MIRV development in 1968 not as a reaction to anything the Soviet Union had done but as a prudent insurance against what they might do in the future.[6] This jumbles the action–reaction sequence so that the reaction precedes the action that is held to justify it.

The equipment requirements generated by long-term threat assessment are magnified by the operation of worst-case analysis. Given imperfect information it is never possible to know exactly what the other side is going to do. If you assume the worst and guess that they will deploy virtually everything they are capable of deploying, then it is necessary to make large deployments yourself to counteract this. If the projected numbers on the other side fail to materialize you have spent more than you needed. You are poor but secure. If you guess too low the adversary ends up a decade hence with greater military assets than you possess. You are richer, but insecure. Given these alternatives defence establishments always prefer to play safe by using worst-case assumptions about what the adversary will do. Invariably this leads to overreaction, with weapons development exceeding what was justified by the actual situation.[7]

On occasion the nature of the 'threat' provokes an immediate scepticism. In 1959 General Dwight Beach assured a Senate subcommittee that the Soviets had to be beaten to the moon because the nation that got there first would have a tremendous military advantage over any enemy. In 1981 the Washington Post revealed a Pentagon programme working on 'psychotechtronic' weapons designed to utilize extra-sensory perception (ESP). Justification for this was the existence of an 'ESP gap' between the US and the Soviet Union. According to the Defence Intelligence Agency the Soviets had already demonstrated telepathic military potential and were also working on 'photonic barrier modulators' which could induce death or illness at long range in the same manner as Haitian voodoo witch doctors.[8]

Of greater concern, however, is the allegation made by several prominent former members of the intelligence and research establishment, that deliberate exaggeration of 'the threat' has been a feature of the advice given to successive presidents. President Eisenhower's science adviser felt that such exaggeration consistently frustrated the President's policies. Herbert York, the first Director of Defense Research and Engineering at the Pentagon, referred to a continuous flow of 'phoney intelligence' from a variety of sources, a point corroborated by Herbert Scoville who directed scientific intelligence for the CIA during the 1960s.[9]

Intelligence estimates are crucial because they help define the nature and scale of the threat. Political leaderships often subscribe to a fairly simplistic action–reaction view of military competition. In the classic statement of this outlook, Robert McNamara argued that 'actions – or even realistically potential actions – on either side relating to the build-up of nuclear forces, be they either offensive or defensive weapons, necessarily trigger reactions on the other side.'[10] This may be seen as the 'rational actor' view of military technological development, one in which estimates of the other side's actual or potential capabilities drives the research and procurement process.

A variation of this explanation is the view that strategic doctrine explains weapon programmes and that the superpowers have acquired particular weapon systems in order to fulfil the specific requirements of their strategic doctrines. Certainly there seems to have been an element of this in the US nuclear build-up, but the relationship has not been a smooth one. Successive US governments have attempted to formulate strategic doctrines based upon expectations about future weapons developments.[11] In a study of US Air Force doctrine published four years before President Reagan's SDI speech, the author noted that US military planners have been 'excessively enamoured of the promise of threshold technology'[12] and tend to ignore evidence that successful military systems emerge from proven technology. Strategic doctrine thus should be a function of availability, but frequently it is not.

During the 1960s the US modified its strategic doctrine at frequent intervals, from 'deterrence-plus-counterforce' (1963) to 'city-avoidance' (1964), 'damage-limitation and assured destruction' (1966) and finally 'assured destruction' alone (1967). However, these doctrinal changes neither produced nor reflected any alteration in the number of nuclear launchers being deployed. The launcher figures were fixed in 1961–2 and deployment went ahead unaffected by doctrinal oscillations.[13]

Neither did the power of the US arsenal reflect doctrine. McNamara's final posture statement laid down that in order to achieve 'assured destruction' of the Soviet Union, 200 Equivalent Megatons (EMTs) would need to be delivered on to Soviet targets. At the time of this statement the US actually possessed 600 EMTs on submarines, 1,000 EMTs on its ICBMs and 4,000 EMTs on its bombers. Even under the most pessimistic assumptions about how many would get through, this represented a vast excess over the necessary megatonnage.[14] Yet no decision to curtail the size of the US force was felt necessary in the light of this enormous overkill.

In the case of the 1960s American build-up, the crucial decisions about the size and nature of the US strategic nuclear forces were taken in the years 1961–2. Two factors drove the build-up: a US intelligence failure in the late 1950s, and the domestic political considerations of President Kennedy.

At the end of the 1950s US intelligence produced indications of a growing 'bomber gap' between the US and USSR. This was followed by a 'missile gap'. These warnings were based upon prototype testing in the USSR, the shock of the 1957 'Sputnik' space launch and clever Soviet propaganda which exaggerated Soviet strength. The issue became a matter of political controversy during the 1960 presidential election, with Senator John F. Kennedy accusing the Eisenhower administration of having allowed the missile gap to develop. The administration rejected these claims but was hampered by a lack of conclusive evidence. During this period satellite reconnaissance had not yet become available, while U-2 reconnaissance aircraft flights over the Soviet Union had been suspended as a result of the shooting down of Gary Powers. As evidence became available in greater quantities it became clear that the missile gap was a myth. However, by then Kennedy, having won a narrow victory partly on allegations of the gap's existence, felt he could not retract and ordered a major nuclear build-up to redress an imbalance which he knew to be non-existent.

What this example demonstrates is that the demand for new weapons is not always generated by genuine threat assessments. Indeed there are strong grounds for believing that the existence of the threat provides a convenient rationale for programmes whose real origins have little if anything to do with the activities of the adversary.

Technology Push

Although it is usual to view military research and development (R and D) as being a reaction to what the other side is doing, or what it might be expected to be doing in future, a great deal of such research is in fact driven by internal rather than external factors. According to Herbert York, 'the arms race is not so much a series of political provocations followed by hot emotional reactions as it is a series of technical challenges followed by cool, calculated responses in the form of ever more costly, more complex and more fully automatic devices.'[15]

Sometimes these technical challenges are generated by the need to compete with the efforts being made in the same field by the opponent; sometimes they are simply the result of the scientists' desire to continually refine and improve and to explore the potential of threshold technology and new concepts. Soviet and US scientists are stimulated to open up new areas of weapons research both by their adversary's efforts and by the new ideas which come to them as they seek to overcome the efforts of their opposite numbers.[16]

An example of the latter impulse was the development of multiple-warhead technology by the US. In 1956 the US began investigating the problems involved in intercepting incoming nuclear ballistic missiles. This programme predated the testing of the first successful ICBM by the Soviet Union. Having begun the Nike–Zeus ABM project to defend against Soviet missiles that had yet to be deployed, the government established a committee to examine the possible countermeasures the Soviets might take in the future to overcome the US ABM network once it was built. The committee noted such technical possibilities as decoys, radar-reflecting 'chaff', lowering the radar profile of warheads, and also the use of multiple warheads on each launcher.[17] What is significant here is that the US was in effect conducting an arms race against itself. The scientists were being driven on by their own professional instincts and their urge to overcome potential problems, problems which were being generated not by the Soviet ABM programme, of which little if anything was known,[18] but by the US ABM programme. This remained the primary rationale throughout the MIRV development. John Foster, who was Director of Defense Research and Engineering during the key period of US MIRV development told Congress that American R and D was driven by essentially internal dynamics. Scientists either see new technical developments which seem worth exploiting, or 'we see threats on the horizon, possible threats, usually not something the enemy has done, but something we have thought of ourselves that he might do, we must therefore be prepared for.'[19]

Scientists are driven by particular motivations and mental pressures. It is part of their mental make-up to want to explore technological frontiers, to find out if a particularly enticing technology will actually work. If there is compelling evidence that the adversary is working along similar lines, so much the better, but even if such evidence is ambiguous or even totally lacking the pressure to explore the limits of the technology is still there. There is a willingness to believe in the threat because it justifies the research. Scientists may even suggest that the other side is working on something because they themselves want to explore that technology. 'Some have sought out and even made up problems to fit the solution they have spent much of their lives discovering and developing.'[20]

By working on such problems, exploring 'sweet' technologies, scientists can create their own realities. Once a new weapon system has been created, even once the relevant technologies have been proven possible, a momentum is generated which sets up almost irresistible pressures in favour of deployment. The secretive nature of military research means that most programmes do not become politically visible until they are considerably advanced. By that stage the basic technology is already largely proven and the armed service likely to obtain the weapon has already become convinced that the new system will fulfil a real military requirement. Political decision-makers have neither the time nor the expertise necessary continually to monitor potential technological developments at the stage when military or civilian vested interests have not yet become fully committed to their exploitation.

It is rare for political leaders to be faced with real choices about weapons development. Their options are shaped by 'trends in military technology that have already been guided by lower level engineers or project managers'.[21] Thus, for example, by the time the wider political and academic community in the US became alert to the dangerous strategic implications of MIRV technology, MIRVed warheads had already been tested, the new missiles to carry them had already gone into production and the conversion of older submarines to carry MIRVed Poseidon missiles was already under way.[22]

In this crucial instance the pace of technological development had already left arms control stranded. Due to the impossibility of distinguishing between MIRVed and single-warhead missiles using satellite photography, once flight-testing of MIRV began a ban on such technology would become virtually impossible because it could not be satisfactorily monitored. To its credit, the Senate was quick to spot the danger, a sub-committee noting that if the US could develop such technology the Soviet Union would soon follow and given that Soviet missiles were larger than their US equivalents, the Soviets could place more warheads atop them. At the end of the day, therefore, proceeding with MIRV would be to the disadvantage of the US.[23] This in fact is exactly what went on to occur during the 1970s. Unfortunately the committee did not recommend a negotiated ban on MIRVs; rather it argued that the US should increase the size of its missiles. Because political pressure against MIRV deployment lagged so far behind the pace of technological advance, the Johnson administration failed to defer flight-testing for a period long enough to determine whether the Soviet Union could be convinced of the need for a mutual ban.[24]

To a significant extent the crucial issues of arms control and security are thus the product of the 'unplanned and unrestrained technological exploitation of new scientific knowledge'.[25] New technologies narrow the options of policy-makers to the point where they have little genuine choice. The rationale for MIRV changed frequently during the 1960s and included such divergent aims as overcoming Soviet ABM defences[26] and increasing the number and variety of targets vulnerable to the US.[27] ABM changed from being a protection against an all-out Soviet attack, a hedge against accidental Soviet launch or a limited Chinese attack, and a protection for a few key ICBM fields. Similarly the goals of SDI have narrowed over time. What is striking is the picture of a technology in search of a mission in each case. Once certain technologies are available their proponents will use almost any rationales, and chop and change between them, to make deployment possible. The weapon system becomes more important than the purpose it is supposed to fulfil.

Some analysts go so far as to suggest that it is the scientists rather than the military who create military needs. They do this as a function of their research, because it is the scientist who tinkers with the potential for devising a new warhead 'and if a new warhead, then a new missile; and, given a new missile, a new system within which it has to fit'.[28] There are without doubt occasions when this is the case; certainly some major programmes such as the US MIRV seem to fit this pattern. It is by no means the whole of the picture, however. The vast majority of weapons systems originate in the expressed needs of the services themselves: either through a desire to have an improved version of the technology they already possess, or through a wish to acquire capabilities they currently lack. The particular problems of static trench warfare in 1915–16 led to the requirement for a vehicle like the tank, and the poor dogfighting capabilities of the F-4

Phantom during the Vietnam War led to the development of the F-15 Eagle during the 1970s.

However, sometimes the activities of the research scientists and the wishes of the armed forces produce irrational weapons development in a manner highly reminiscent of the pattern suggested by Lord Zuckerman above. For example, in 1973 it was announced that when the first US Trident submarines became operational they would be based near Bangor, Washington State, on America's northern Pacific coastline. At first sight there seemed little if any logic in such a decision. The justification for the Trident programme was that a longer-range missile would give the Poseidon-class submarines larger patrol areas to operate from and thereby reduce the likelihood of their being detected by the Soviets. However, by basing them on the Pacific this advantage was lost since the majority of targets are west of the Urals; in order to reach them from the Pacific the submarines would have to operate in a restricted patrol-area in the north-west Pacific. Moreover, to reach the open seas from their base the submarines would have to negotiate a narrow strait in international waters, an ideal place for Soviet submarine detection devices to be emplaced. From the point of view of US national interests, therefore, the choice of Bangor as a base made little sense.

From the narrow sectional interests of the US Navy and the missile and submarine design teams, the Bangor decision nevertheless made all the sense in the world. Precisely because the Trident-I (C-4) missiles range would force the boats close to the USSR the Navy would be able to press the need for the longer-range follow-on Trident-II (D-5) missile. Unlike the C-4, the D-5 was too large to be retrofitted on to existing Poseidon boats so a new, larger class of SSBN would be required. Thus the navy would get large new submarines and missiles and the design teams would be kept busy. A political factor was also relevant. The influential Senator Henry Jackson, a hawk on defence issues, voted against the proposed Trident programme in the Armed Services Committee in 1972. Senator Jackson represented Washington State. After it was announced that the base (with all its job-creation potential) would be situated in his own state Senator Jackson's jaundiced views on the Trident programme became positively rose-tinted. In 1973 he not only voted in favour of it, but became its most ardent advocate.[29]

Interpretations such as this suggest that while threat-perception and the actions of the international adversary are clearly significant, the superpowers' military inventories are 'predominantly the result of factors internal to each nation'[30] and that therefore a true understanding of the obstacles in the way of effective arms control necessitates recognizing the impact of national weapons acquisition processes.[31]

The US Weapons Acquisition Process

The very wealth and inventive genius of the US causes continual problems for arms control. Politicians come and go but the research scientists have a continuity of impact denied their political and military masters. In a wealthy society with a 'can do' mentality neither resource constraints nor technological obstacles act as natural limitations upon effort to the extent that they do in other countries. It has been argued that America's problem has not been in getting the weapons it wants, but rather avoiding those it does not want or need.[32]

There are a number of reasons why this is the case. America is a society in love with technology, and moreover one with a disturbing tendency to believe that political problems are susceptible to technological solutions. The idea of continual technological progress is built into US self-belief. In the twentieth century this attitude has brought both the unprecedented prosperity enjoyed by the US and the unparalleled insecurity of the nuclear era. In this sense the guiding outlook of the weapons scientists reflects that of society as a whole.

Furthermore, the US since 1945 has consistently relied upon technological supremacy to offset numerical disadvantages in the military competition with the Soviet Union. With technology having a driving affect on the arms race this need to maintain the leading position has necessarily meant that it has usually been the US which has been the initiator of technological competition. This has been particularly evident in the past 15 years as quality rather than quantity has become the definitive criteria for success in the nuclear arms race. It is therefore difficult for the US to take a favourable view of qualitative (as distinct from quantitative) constraints upon its forces, as was demonstrated by the refusal of the Reagan administration to join the Soviet moratorium on nuclear testing in 1986.

However, this suspicion of constraints on technological progress in weapons development poses genuine problems for future arms control. Such constraints are difficult even to formulate and they certainly cannot work if one side wishes to see technology left unconstrained.[33] Yet it is argued that the next generation of strategic nuclear weapons will be incapable of being limited by treaty once deployed, and that 'modern technology eliminates the prospects for arms control.'[34] Many of the new weapon systems would be not only difficult to monitor, but would have a negative impact upon strategic stability.[35] This is true both of increasingly accurate ballistic missiles and of possible strategic defences.

The weapons development process in the US favours technical complexity and this has meant that the technologically oriented services have been significantly more successful in the struggle over the years on budgetary allocations. This is particularly true of the Air Force.[36] Weapons acquisition occurs as an output of bureaucratic politics and there is a tendency towards compromise which benefits all the services. Thus in the 1970s the simultaneous programmes on the B-1 bomber, MX ICBM, Trident SLBM and Pershing 2 missile kept all the services happy.

The continuous R and D process noted earlier creates its own pressures. The existence of large organizations whose only justification for existing is the ability to 'design new weapons and sell them to political decision-makers'[37] means that there is a constant supply of developments looking for a role. As noted earlier, by the time these become politically visible the programmes have acquired such momentum that they are very difficult to stop. By 1972, with the signing of the SALT I ABM treaty, the US MIRV programme had produced several rationales yet the treaty demolished its ultimate rationale, the need to penetrate a nationwide Soviet ABM system. Logically, therefore, the MIRV programme could and should have been abandoned in 1972. In practice it carried on regardless and it did so because of the dead hand of bureaucratic inertia. To have abandoned the programme by that stage would have meant overcoming the noisy objections of a large lobby whose support of MIRV had always transcended the rationales for the system. Neither Nixon nor Kissinger were prepared for the bruising battle this would involve, so MIRVing went ahead.[38]

Other weapon systems may be justified and yet again have a suspicion of irrationality attached to the precise nature of their place
in the force posture. The US is committed to the maintenance of
carrier battle-groups, each one centred around the enormously
powerful nuclear powered aircraft-carriers. During the 1960s the 15
large aircraft-carriers required by the US Navy were justified in
terms of the Kennedy 'two and a half war capability' that is the ability
to be able to fight two major and one minor wars simultaneously. By
the 1970s the US had opted for a 'a one and a half war capability', yet
the 15 carrier requirement remained unaltered. Reasonable
arguments can be advanced for having the flexibility represented by
these nuclear carrier assets, yet it is curious that 15 was also the
number of capital ships allotted to the US by the 1921 Washington
Naval Disarmament Treaty. Since 1921 the US Navy has always
maintained 15 capital ships in peacetime, despite all the intervening
changes in technology, missions and international politics. It may be
purely coincidence, but one cannot help suspecting that there is a
deeper *gestalt* at work. Actions by the adversary may therefore play
only a tangential role in justifying weapon systems that the military
bureaucracies favour for all sorts of other reasons.

It is not simply military bureaucracies which generate weapons,
such as the cruise missile, without any well-defined picture of what
they are needed for; the relationship between the civilian defence
firms and the political establishment in the US has the same auton-
omous impact. Thus when a particular company reaches the end of a
production run of an existing weapon-system it invariably begins
producing a new one within a year. The contracts for the new system
– which is a more modern, technically superior product in the same
category as the one previously produced – is normally signed two to
three years before a production run ends. The new contract is therefore a 'follow-on' contract. Such contracts preserve design teams
intact, maintain employment levels and perpetuate certain skills.
They may also help the re-election of the local congressman. They do
not always produce a product that is genuinely needed, however. As
James Kurth has noted, 'it is not always obvious that there should be
any new system at all in an old production section.'[39] The experience
with systems such as the B-1 bomber and the F-18 fighter seem to
bear this out. Yet pork-barrel democratic politics ensures that such
follow-on contracts are a feature of the weapons development process.

Given the military and congressional momentum behind particular weapons programmes it is hardly surprising, for example, that a 1977 Library of Congress study found that the arms control impact statements submitted to Congress by the Ford administration were 'biased in favour of producing the weapons in question'.[40]

The Soviet Weapons Development Process

The weapons development process in the USSR differs in a number of ways from its US counterpart, though there are also many similarities. As with the US there has been a tendency to try to anticipate and emulate the weapons produced by the adversary. US–Soviet competition is such that they rarely try to match systems; rather the relationship is one in which systems counter each other. Thus US bomber advances produced Soviet interceptor efforts rather than a parallel bomber programme. Submarines and anti-submarine warfare, tanks and anti-tank weapons show a similar relationship.

As with the US the general nature of the development process is driven by both internal and external forces. Examples of Soviet efforts to counter US systems are not hard to find. Thus, for example, the specific performance capabilities of the MiG-25 were clearly based upon a desire to counter the B-70 supersonic high-altitude bomber. The latter in fact never went into production, but the MiG-25 emerged nevertheless. This demonstrates that the Soviet Union is not immune to the problem of producing weapons it does not really need, though in general terms resource constraints usually make it easier for the USSR to avoid getting what it does not want. Conversely, however, it has relatively more difficulty in obtaining precisely what it needs.[41]

Like those in the US the Soviet planners work on the basis of worst-case assumptions, and likewise too they tend to base their assumptions about what the adversary is likely to do upon knowledge of the areas being explored by Soviet defence scientists.[42] To this extent the Soviet Union races against itself. However, the Soviets are also driven by a profound respect for the potential of US technology. It was notable in the ABM debates of the early 1970s and mid-1980s that however sceptical Western scientific opinion was of the likelihood of US breakthroughs, the Soviet leadership did not want to take the risk that the US might achieve the apparently impossible.

The Soviet system, by contrast, tends to produce steady incremental progress in technology rather than the quantum leaps occasionally achieved by the US. This is not to belittle the achievements of Soviet science and technology. On the contrary, their space programme has been eloquent testimony to how much can be achieved by this approach. However, it is a matter of simple observation that in the Soviet Union the approach taken to design and development tends to minimize technological advances in successive generations, an approach which carries both advantages and disadvantages.

Centralized decision-making is a feature of the Soviet procurement system. The Deputy Minister of Defence for Armaments has the responsibility for coordinating the procurement process and this has the beneficial effect of reducing the impact of inter-service rivalry.[43] This does not mean that service imput is less important however. In the Soviet system the absence of market forces places a premium upon early and detailed product definition by the consumer: that is, the potential operating service.

In order to produce reliable designs the Soviets emphasize the prototype system in a way that the US does not. Whereas the USAF ordered 100 B1-B bombers before the first had been test-flown and then found that those delivered operated well below requirements, Soviet designers eliminate weaknesses through successive prototypes. Ironically in some ways, there is more genuine competition in the Soviet system than in the American. Prior to a decision on production several design bureaux will submit prototypes which will then be subject to an intense competition. Competitive evaluation is a central feature of Soviet weapons procurement.[44] There also appear to be differences between the US and Soviet weapon specification approaches. Whereas in the US the service in question provides a manufacturer with a list of capabilities which the weapon is supposed to be built to perform, in the Soviet Union the actual performance of the prototype will determine its military value. This is particularly true of the aircraft industry.

Soviet designers go for simplicity of design, the use of components common to other equipment and an evolutionary approach to weapons development. These criteria reduce the amount of technological innovation involved in any new design but have the compensating benefits of reducing the size and time-scale of development programmes, which has the effect of holding down costs.[45] Designers tend to prefer to improve existing designs rather than attempt to achieve design breakthroughs.

The preference for simple, comparatively inexpensive, military technology enabled the Soviet Union to build up a marked numerical advantage over NATO in many weapons categories, and a statement attributed to Khrushchev asserted that 'quantity has a quality of its own.'[46] It is becoming increasingly difficult for the Soviet Union to avoid being drawn into the hi-tech arena, however. As Soviet weapon systems become more advanced, such as the MiG-29 and MiG-31 aircraft, so the Soviet acquisition pattern is becoming more like the American, with lower rates of production and smaller numbers produced. The output of Soviet conventional weaponry has declined significantly since the late 1970s for this very reason. The final 5 per cent of weapons performance is disproportionately costly to achieve.

Although central planning is such a feature of Soviet life, R and D projects on a massive scale (analogous to the Manhattan Project of the Second World War) have not been a feature of the Soviet practice. The tenacious way in which Soviet government ministries defend their areas of responsibility against incursions acts as an effective barrier to large-scale inter-ministerial projects. In addition narrowly focused projects tend to soak up scarce resources and throw innumerable less-favoured programmes into disarray. Nevertheless, such major programmes have been deemed necessary on occasion, particularly when it is felt crucial to close a particular technological gap with the West as quickly as possible. The Soviet response to the US MIRV programme seems to fit this pattern.[47] The Soviet ICBM build-up after 1963 also seems to have been a rushed overreaction caused by the US build-up that began three years earlier.[48] The establishment of a special purpose agency to cross existing institutional boundaries when a technological crisis is perceived has been used before,[49] and it is highly likely that the Soviet reaction to SDI has been to effect a consolidating programme of this sort.

Soviet weapons acquisition seems to be just as prone to irrational decisions prompted by organizational politics as are US decisions. The case of the unnecessary MiG-25 has already been noted. During the 1950s the Soviet Union deployed huge numbers of MiG-17 and MiG-19 interceptors. These aircraft were only capable of operating in daylight. A more logical acquisition programme would have acquired somewhat fewer of these aircraft, freeing funds to develop interceptors with a night-time capability. However, PVO–Strany the Soviet air-defence force had just been made a separate organization and wanted to spend all its generous new annual budget rather than limit itself in order to free funds for other worthy purposes.

Civilian science does not appear to be a major factor in the Soviet weapons acquisition process. The overwhelming majority of military R and D is done within the Defence Ministry itself or within the military production ministries, although a small-scale but developing symbiotic relationship does exist. Nearly half the institutes in the Academy of Sciences have done some military research in the past two decades and, in an era of economic retrenchment, the huge size of the military budget acts as a magnet to civilian scientists and research teams exactly as it does in the West.[50] Moreover several ministerial posts have traditionally been filled by scientists or engineers. However, the kind of research done by civilian groups for military purposes appears to be limited to early problem correction rather than long-term input into the development process.

Certain Soviet programmes appear to be opportunistic, but these can have profound political implications. The Soviet ASAT programme appears to have been pursued without a well-defined concept of why they were needed and without regard to the diplomatic implications of their development. As with the US MIRV the sweetness of the technology was all. Satellite rendezvous techniques were available and so was a redundant launcher, the SS-9, and the two were brought together to see what their military potential was. The programme does not appear to have a high priority since it has been suspended during periods when good relations with the US were at a premium. Similarly the SS-16 ICBM flight-tested in the early 1970s proved a disaster due to the poor performance of the first-stage booster. The Soviet Union, making a virtue of necessity, deployed the top two stages as an intermediate-range ballistic missile to replace the ageing SS-4s and SS-5s in Europe. NATO codenamed the two-stage version the SS-20 and its arrival provoked an arms race in medium-range nuclear missiles in Europe. With occasional exceptions such as these, however, weapons deployment in the Soviet Union originates more from a 'requirements pull' than from a 'technology push'.

Ballistic Missile Defence Technologies

A case-study of technological determinism in the arms race defining the limits of arms control can be seen in the search for an effective defence against ballistic missiles over the past 30 years.

Considerations of ballistic missile defence technologies began almost immediately after the development of ballistic missiles. In 1947 General Walter Dornberger, who had directed the German V-2 missile project during the Second World War, moved to the US to work as a consultant for the Defence Department. Almost immediately he produced a paper outlining a proposal for an ABM system orbiting in space. The system was based upon a network of satellites armed with heat-seeking missiles.[51] The proposal was subsequently adopted by the USAF as Project BAMBI (Ballistic Missile Boost Intercept).

Major research into BMD began in the US in 1957. In that year the Soviet Union flight-tested its first ICBM. The Eisenhower administration reacted by initiating two BMD research programmes. The first attempted to utilize existing technology and investigated the potential for upgrading the Nike anti-aircraft missile to give it an anti-missile capability. The second programme, codenamed Project Defender, looked at the ABM potential of new techniques and technologies. Project Defender was initiated in 1958 and involved thousands of scientists and a multi-million dollar budget.[52]

During the 1960s the US continued to work on ABM defences although the results obtained from the research programme were persistently discouraging. President Kennedy cancelled the Nike–Zeus ground-based missile system because of its poor potential. This system relied on mechanically steered radars to guide a missile armed with a high-yield nuclear warhead. A 1962 test of such a device revealed the existence of the hitherto unsuspected nuclear-induced electromagnetic pulse (NEMP). The NEMP knocked out the sensitive electronics of all the US satellites above the horizon and caused bizarre atmospheric effects across the Pacific. This led scientists to estimate that a small number of nuclear explosions high in the atmosphere above the US would suffice to neutralize all electronically-based systems on the ground below, from communications networks to car ignition systems.

In 1967 the US scaled down its ambitions. Rather than defend its population against a full-scale Soviet attack, a limited capability against accidental launches, limited Soviet strikes, or a Chinese attack was sought. This system, codenamed Sentinel by the Johnson administration, involved two missiles based on technology evolved from Nike–Zeus. A long-range interceptor, Spartan, was designed to intercept beyond the atmosphere, while a short-range, high-acceleration missile, Sprint, would intercept warheads during the re-entry phase. A modern phased-array radar would guide the missiles to their targets.

When the Nixon administration came into office in 1969 it reduced the objectives of US BMD still further. The Sentinel technology, renamed Safeguard, was given the task of defending US retaliatory capability rather than its population. Safeguard finally became operational on 1 April 1975, defending the ICBM fields at Grand Forks in North Dakota.

The reasons for the minimal US BMD deployment were partly political and partly technological. There was domestic political opposition to a system that offered no defence to the US population and yet was vastly expensive. Shortly after the $7 billion Safeguard ABM site became operational, Congress voted to close it down again and it was deactivated in 1976. In addition, between 1969 and 1975 the international political situation had changed, leading to the 1972 US–Soviet ABM Treaty which limited each side to two ABM sites, each with 100 interceptors. A 1974 protocol to the treaty reduced this to a single permitted site each. President Nixon had come to the conclusion that a major ABM deployment might appear to the Soviet Union as a prelude to an offensive strategy. As Bernard Brodie replied to Herman Kahn's assertion that 'if we deploy a full-scale anti-ballistic missile system, we can save 50 million lives', in order to save 50 million lives you have got to have a war.[53] The Nixon administration felt that even the widest ABM deployment considered could not prevent 'catastrophic' US casualty levels in the event of a nuclear war with the Soviet Union.

President Nixon's calculations were based upon the technological inadequacies of the Safeguard system. Its radars were extremely vulnerable to attack: the guidance systems were not particularly sophisticated; its capability to distinguish between warheads and decoys was limited; and it relied upon nuclear warheads to destroy the target. Calculations indicated that it would be far more expensive for the US to improve its defences than it would be for the Soviet Union to overcome such improvements.

Despite the ABM treaty and the deactivation of the Grand Forks site, research into improving ICBM defence by ABMs continued, although congressional restrictions limited the programme to component development and forbade the testing of prototypes. The technology developed formed the basis of the Low Altitude Defense System (LOADS) which was assessed as a protection for MX missile silos in the early 1980s.

The major defect of all the ground-based interception technologies was their inability to attack Soviet ICBMs in their boost-phase immediately after launch when they can be destroyed prior to releasing any of their multiple warheads or associated decoys. Interception in the boost phase requires the destruction of some 2,000 targets. By the terminal and mid-course phases envisaged in Safeguard, the number of possible targets is over half a million. Space-based interceptors were investigated during the 1980s in the Overlay programme. By 1983, when President Reagan made his famous 'Star Wars' speech, developments in technologies such as computers, integrated circuits, target discrimination and directed energy meant that the possibility of boost-phase interception seemed worthy of a major research effort for the first time. As early as 1978 George Rathjens correctly predicted that 'as soon as these technologies produce an ABM system that appears feasible, there will be instantaneous, strong pressure to modify or abrogate the 1972 treaty and deploy a system.'[54]

The US BMD programme illustrates many of the features of the interaction between technological progress and politics in weapons development. There has, since the development of the reality of mutual assured destruction in the 1950s, existed a school of thought which believes that it is only prudent to attain the ability to defend against a nuclear attack. A situation of perfect defence is so inherently attractive that from time to time US governments have experienced bursts of enthusiasm for major research programmes in this field. Even when the outcome has been disappointing, or when administrations less enamoured of the defensive concept have been in office, it has still been thought necessary to continue with low-key programmes of research into new technological possibilities in case one or several of these should provide a breakthrough in BMD capabilities. These programmes continually push back the frontiers of knowledge, changing the status quo and presenting new administrations with engineering capabilities which seem to require reassessment of earlier attitudes towards the viability of BMD. Technological advance changes political realities by altering perceptions of what is possible. It is this which has led critics of the impact of military R and D to argue that there can be no genuine control over the momentum of the arms race unless ways are found of constraining military R and D.[55]

The Problem of Control

The problem with controlling advances in knowledge of military technology is that it is impossible to achieve. As Lord Zuckerman has noted, 'No one can ban what is not yet discovered. It is impossible to put the unknown into chains. At every moment the future is at the mercy of some discovery not yet made.'[56] This is all the more so because military technology is not always the result of research into weaponry. The modern bomber and jet fighter developed out of early civilian experiments in heavier-than-air flying machines. Halting progress in military technology would have to mean halting *all* development: no new medicines, improved computers, space rockets, aircraft radars, ship turbines, laser surgery and so on. Almost any development can be used to improve a military capability. A complete ban on all technological progress would not be desirable even if it were feasible, which it is not.

It is also important to remember that technological progress is not always the enemy of arms control. The same advances in satellite technology that improved missile targeting and battle-management capabilities during the 1960s also made possible a plethora of arms control agreements, thanks to remove verification by satellite. It is also true that the purposes of arms control are sometimes served by the advent of new weaponry. This was the case with the deployment of SSBNs in the 1960s. The latter case also shows that the same development can be both a gain and a loss simultaneously. Nuclear-missile submarines aided strategic stability (an arms control objective) by being invulnerable, second-strike systems, but they were also inherently difficult to monitor by satellite. A system like the Midgetman or SS-25 mobile ICBM poses all sorts of dilemmas for arms control. It is more survivable than its predecessor, which is good, but harder to monitor, which is bad. Its smaller warhead means less collateral damage if war breaks out, which is good, but might thereby reduce the disincentives to going to war in the first place, which is bad. It has been argued that any strategic system which can be monitored for arms control purposes must therefore (because of modern weapon accuracies) be vulnerable to a first strike.[57]

Technological development is also difficult to ban because to a large extent it *is* the superpower nuclear arms race. Since nuclear weapons cannot actually be used in order to demonstrate one side's superiority, competition in numbers and quality of weaponry has served as a surrogate trial of strength. In addition the broader competition is the modern manifestation of strategic manoeuvre. 'Nowadays instead of manoeuvering soldiers over areas of ground, strategic adversaries manoeuver scientific and industrial potentials over periods of time.'[58]

This does not mean that there is no scope for limitations upon technological development. Once weapons systems have developed beyond the research stage they can be identified and may be seen as candidates for constraint. During the SALT I negotiations the Soviet delegate Semyenov argued that it would be sensible 'to prevent the deployment of types of strategic offensive armaments capable of significantly affecting the further development of the arms race, as well as types possibly not possessed by the sides at the present time, but which, if made operational, could lead to an intensification of the arms race.'[59]

Prior to deployment there is always the opportunity to limit or forestall deployment through negotiations. NATO attempted to do this in 1979 by offering not to deploy any cruise or Pershing 2 missiles if the Soviet Union would drastically reduce its own INF missiles. The USSR did not take up the offer. With both MIRV and cruise technology, the consequences of the failure to limit prior to deployment were an intensified arms race and significantly diminished security for both sides.

It is difficult to constrain weapons programmes at the predeployment phase because the two sides are only very rarely synchronized when it comes to deployment. With MIRV, for example, the US was several years ahead of the Soviet Union and would have had to give up this advantage to achieve a MIRV ban. Similarly, in 1979 the Soviet Union was unwilling to give up the monopoly of intermediate-range nuclear ballistic missiles it enjoyed at the time. The 1972 ABM treaty was possible because the two sides had tradeable advantages: the USSR had an existing, but primitive, system, the US had the momentum to deploy a system more capable than the Soviet one fairly quickly. A deal was therefore possible, but it still took three years to negotiate.

With many technologies there is a limited 'window of opportunity' for constraint. Congress prevented full-scale testing of the US ASAT in the mid-1980s because of the realization that once the system was proven in space, verification of a ban would become immensely more complicated. Similarly, with MIRV the opportunity for a complete ban only existed prior to the first flight-tests of MIRVed missiles.

If development cannot always be prevented it may be slowed or channelled in such a way as to improve the chances of arms control keeping pace with technology. A ban, or even severe numerical limitations, upon the flight-testing of ICBMs would slow the development of new types and introduce an element of doubt regarding the effectiveness of existing ones, thereby reducing the likelihood of a first strike using such weapons. A complete ban or even reduced-yield threshold for nuclear test explosions would likewise complicate the development of new warheads and reduce confidence in the existing stockpile by a small but useful degree, whereas a complete ban on test explosions during the 1970s would not have been an unmitigated benefit since the tests allowed significant reductions in warhead yields producing a fall in overall megatonnage, and a reduction in maximum allowed yields now would reinforce this trend. Limitations on testing of systems would also be useful. It is often the case that while elements of a system in themselves work well enough, they cannot be integrated successfully into a working system. Constraining the ability to test complete systems would drastically reduce confidence in the system as a whole. Limitations on the testing of components and systems remain the most promising avenue for constraining the qualitative arms race.

Conclusions

Putting limits on the qualitative arms race has proven extremely difficult in the past because of the nature of research and the asymmetry in programme development between the superpowers.

Currently, however, qualitative changes threaten stability far more than numerical variations. A significant point for the arms control community is that much, if not most, of the momentum generating technology push appears to be autarchic: that is, it is the product of the internal dynamics of domestic institutions rather than a rational response to the actions of the adversary. Recognition of this, in the manner of Congress restraining US ASAT development, might enable future windows of opportunity to be held open long enough for constraining arms control agreements to be negotiated within them. In this area unilateral restraint is crucially important to the potential for success of arms control.

4

The Economic
Implications of Arms
Control

The economic problems of disarmament are not so grave that they
should be allowed to influence our attitude toward armaments.
Benoit, 'The Economic Impact of Disarmament in the United States'[1]

In matters concerning arms control, the object of saving money really
deserves a superior rating to that of saving the world.
Brodie, *How Much is Enough? Guns versus Butter Revisited*[2]

Introduction

Economic arguments have not been pivotal in the debates about arms
control in the northern hemisphere to date. The simple reason for this
is that since the arms control achieved so far has been small scale and
lacking in real impact on virile military systems, there has been no
need to worry greatly about any economic implications it might have.
Why then is it necessary to address the subject at all?

The economics of arms control and disarmament are worthy of
study for a number of reasons. For one thing there is a school of
thought which argues that it is the political power wielded by those
who make large profits from the arms industry which explains why
there has been so little disarmament to date. In addition to those who
profit from weapons production there are those who are employed in
the arms industry who also have a vested interest in the maintenance
of high levels of arms production. Even when the more modest goal of
arms control is being pursued, it is noticeable that levels of arms
spending tend to remain high even when certain programmes are cut

back, because defence spending tends to be rechannelled into other, unconstrained areas. Any arms control or disarmament strategy which fails to take these economic implications into account, therefore, is unlikely to be politically acceptable.

A broader argument is that regarding the impact of defence spending upon the health of the economy. Here there is a clear division between those who argue, on *economic* grounds, that defence spending helps economic growth[3] and those who argue that it hinders it.[4]

In the event of major disarmament occurring, along the lines of that proposed by both superpowers at the Reykjavik meeting in October 1986, then large-scale conversion of some weapons companies' production lines would be necessary and so the likely difficulties of such 'conversion' programmes need to be thought about in advance. Another major source of controversy is the argument over whether major disarmament would automatically trigger an economic recession, perhaps even a depression. Finally the economic impact upon Soviet-style 'command economies' needs to be looked at.

The Danger of Depression

An analysis by a US economist of his country's historical experience, published in 1960, seemed to show that significant reductions in defence spending lead inevitably to economic recession. This pattern was seen after the end of the war of 1812, the Civil War and the First World War. In addition the depression of the 1930s was a period of low spending on defence and, while after seven years of 'New Deal' economics US unemployment in 1940 was still at 17 per cent, after three years of war it fell from 9.5 million to 1 million.[5] Again, during the Eisenhower presidency when defence spending was sharply cut back, recession followed and unemployment rose.

Contradictory evidence emerges from the experience after the Second World War, however. In both the US and Britain defence spending was cut dramatically after 1945 and enormous numbers of demobilized soldiers returned to the job market. Yet unemployment remained low and a period of economic boom rather than recession followed, so that it could be argued that on the basis of British and US experience after 1945 'a disarmament programme of considerably greater proportions than would now be necessary can be carried out without causing a major upset to the economy as a whole.'[6]

The key to the different effects of peace in 1919 and 1945 lay in the nature of aggregate demand in the economy. A look at the situation in 1945 makes clear the processes at work. In June 1945 there were some 9 million people involved in the British war effort, either in the armed forces or in war production. By December 1946, when demobilization was completed, 4.3 million soldiers had returned to civilian life and 3.5 million people had left their jobs in the war industries.[7] In just 18 months nearly 8 million people had entered the labour market, yet they were able to find jobs and unemployment remained low in 1946 and 1947.[8] In the US over a similar period 9 million men were demobilized, yet unemployment remained below 4 per cent.

The economies of Britain and the US remained buoyant in 1945 for a number of reasons. In 1945 there was an enormous pent-up demand in these countries for goods that had been rationed or even unobtainable in wartime. People had plenty of money to pay for these goods because during the war there had been few luxuries available to spend their money on. Thus when peace came factories were kept busy coping with this recently released demand; people could afford to pay for the goods produced and the producers needed lots of labour to meet the demand. All these factors meant that there was no recession and unemployment stayed low. The latter aspect was further helped by the fact that many people who had entered the job market during the war, such as women brought in to work in the factories, voluntarily left the job market in 1945, freeing their jobs for the returning soldiers.

Demand remained high for other reasons also. Britain in 1945 was a country ravaged by war. Enormous destruction had been wrought by the German air force, and the building industry (which is labour-intensive) experienced a dramatic increase in activity.

However, some of these factors were present after earlier wars when recession did occur, or when the post-war boom was of a far briefer and shallower type. One other crucial factor was present in 1945: planning, and particularly the planning associated with interventionist governments. The wartime governments in Britain and the US anticipated the dangers of a post-war recession and therefore made plans to offset the difficulties. This was particularly true in Britain. It was clear that once the vast sums associated with the war effort ceased to pour into the economy a recession would occur unless aggregate demand was maintained by offsetting civilian expenditure to replace the lost defence spending. As noted already, the government's task was made far easier by the huge liquid reserves released into the economy from the private sector after 1945 and by the clear need for the rebuilding of the war-damaged national infrastructure.

The crucial point, therefore, is that defence expenditure has no magical economic properties. Government spending will stimulate economic activity regardless. The experience of the first half of the 1940s created the myth that the massive arms build-up associated with the Second World War ended the depression. The reality, however, is that the $80 billion spent on defence by the US in 1941 was money that would have ended the depression whatever it was spent on.

In the absence of offsetting expenditure, cuts in defence spending will lead to depression of aggregate demand in the economy. Moreover, because of the multiplier effect, the fall in demand is likely to be double the value of the initial reduction in defence spending.

An example of this effect is the experience of the US during the Eisenhower presidency. From 1953 to 1960 real defence spending was reduced by 30 per cent. However, non-defence spending was not increased to make up for this; on the contrary, it too was cut by some 30 per cent in this period. The effect on the economy was disastrous: unemployment doubled and the growth rate fell to one-third of what it had been in the period between 1945 and 1953.[9]

Disarmament does not automatically lead to recession therefore, but sharp reductions in government expenditure do, whether in the military or the civilian sector, as was clearly demonstrated by the performance of the British economy during the first half of the 1980s. In 1962 a UN study concluded that disarmament would not lead to economic slowdown so long as the lost defence spending was replaced by other government expenditure.[10] Significant arms reduction agreements should therefore be accompanied by changes in a government's macro-economic policies to generate additional compensatory demand in the economy.

The Impact on Employment

In political terms, the likely impact upon employment figures is the most crucial economic indicator in determining the acceptability of arms reductions. In the UK for example, large-scale defence cuts have frequently been opposed on the grounds that they would generate unemployment. Government ministers opposed calls for a £1 billion defence cut in 1975 on the grounds that such a move would cost 350,000 jobs.[11] During the 1983 General Election campaign the opposition Labour Party advocated a reduction of British defence spending from 5 per cent of GNP to 3.5 per cent, to bring it into line with the average spending of its European NATO allies. The proposal turned out to be an electoral albatross as the Labour party proved incapable of protecting itself against the Conservative government's claims that a 1.5 per cent fall in defence effort would increase unemployment by 400,000. The Labour Party's failure to win the argument is surprising both because the government's attack was predictable and because the overwhelming weight of evidence contradicts the Conservative claims in 1983. While it is a common assumption that disarmament creates unemployment, existing studies fail to support this belief;[12] indeed, a number of studies indicate that military spending itself generates unemployment.[13]

The argument that defence spending generates rather than reduces unemployment is based on the fact that the defence industry is extremely capital-intensive.[14] Modern military technology is highly complex and specialized so that the rate of cost inflation for defence equipment has been running far in advance of that of civilian equipment for the past two decades. For this reason equivalent levels of government spending generate more employment in the civilian than in the defence sector of the economy.

It is therefore disingenuous to claim, as Defense Secretary Caspar Weinberger did in 1982, that 'you get 35,000 more jobs for every extra $1 billion you spend on national defense.'[15] While Weinberger if anything underestimated the jobs created by such spending, more importantly he failed to point out that far more jobs would be created by a similar injection of funding into the civilian economy. Thus, for example, a 1976 US Bureau of Labour study estimated that for every one billion dollars of government spending 75,000 jobs could be created in defence, compared with 100,000 in the construction industry, 112,000 in consumer goods, 138,000 in health and 187,000 in education.[16]

In assessing the employment effect of defence the key variable is once again the degree of compensatory government spending. A 1983 study of the likely effects on the British economy indicated that a fall in defence spending of one billion pounds would increase unemployment by 150,000 within 12 months, with a further 50,000 jobs being lost over the succeeding four years. With compensatory government spending, however, the same five-year period would see a gain of 125,000 public sector jobs and 130,000 private sector jobs.[17]

Defence spending is less efficient than civilian spending as an employment generator; indeed, a comparative study of the major western economies for the period 1960–79 concluded that 'higher levels of military spending generally correspond with greater unemployment among western industrial nations.'[18]

However, while the employment effects of disarmament are not especially traumatic for the economy as a whole, specific communities may be particularly hard hit because they are disproportionately reliant upon defence spending. This may be because there are military bases sited there or because they are a key centre for the production of military material for which the demand is falling. Defence production employment tends to be particularly concentrated in certain industries (for example, aircraft and shipbuilding) which in turn tend to be concentrated in certain geographical areas. Thus a reduction in the size of the Royal Navy would have marginal effects on British employment totals overall, but the distress caused would be disproportionately concentrated in a small number of communities around the rivers Tyne, Clyde and Mersey. Similarly, the abandonment of a British helicopter manufacturing capability would be a tremendous blow to the town of Yeovil.

In the same way defence production cutbacks have a disproportionate impact on certain vocational groups. The job experience of many engineers, scientists and managers in defence is highly specialized, so specialized in fact that it is extremely difficult for them to adapt to the quite different requirements of the civilian economy; consequently, to a great extent such specialists inevitably find themselves locked 'into a political commitment to the arms race and to its supporting technical and production activity'.[19]

A key feature of any commitment to significant defence cutbacks would therefore have to be a planned programme of conversion and retraining, in order to create new employment opportunities in localities previously dependent upon defence production and to give new skills to those whose careers had previously been limited to the arcane requirements of national security. This view is not universally held. Benoit argued in 1962 for a *laissez-faire* attitude to conversion, insisting that it is not necessary to work out in advance the details of what a particular factory should convert to or where each worker should go in search of a new job, because in a free market economy much of this will happen spontaneously as businesses seek new markets and workers new jobs. [20]

In practice, however, a free market approach is not likely to suffice for a number of reasons. It depends very much upon what the state of the national and international economy is at the time. If there is already a vast degree of overproduction in a market, as with shipping in the 1980s, then a new firm entering the market which previously specialized in warship construction is likely to struggle. Similarly, in an economy marked by very high unemployment someone with highly specialized skills peculiar to a defence-related industry will find it hard to compete for available jobs with those whose experience is more directly relevant.

A planned programme of conversion and retraining can overcome these problems. As long ago as 1931 a committee of the British Transport and General Workers' Union (TGWU) argued that such a programme had to accompany any disarmament breakthrough. The TGWU advised that workers made redundant should be offered alternative employment; that those with skills which could not easily be transferred should be given adequate financial compensation; and that the government should take measures to stimulate alternative employment in the areas worst hit by the defence run-down. [21]

There are a variety of ways in which this last objective might be achieved. These include encouraging the labour force to move to new areas where labour is in demand, encouraging new firms to move into the area where defence production is being run down, or encouraging firms to convert from defence to civilian production in their original location.

The first option suffers from a number of drawbacks. If large numbers of displaced workers are being encouraged to move then their families must accompany them if the integrity of the family unit is to be maintained. This will mean that the existing infrastructure of the new area – housing, schools, hospitals and so on – will come under increased pressure. Local or central government may well be forced to respond to this with new infrastructural investment. At the same time, however, the existing infrastructure in the workers' area of origin will be becoming increasingly underutilized and uneconomic as the local population deserts the area in search of work. An illogical allocation of resources will thus be occurring as one area runs down and another area has to be expensively built up because of the migration of families who never wanted to move in the first place.

This problem can be overcome if the labour force can be retained in its area of origin by providing jobs in that region. One possible way to do this is by regional aid policies which make it attractive for firms to move into such areas. Policies of this sort are in fact practised by a number of governments trying to overcome the problems of declining older industries. It is worth noting the fact that the kinds of economic problem associated with defence cutbacks are a normal part of economic life. There are always some areas particularly hit by the decline of an industry they had depended on; factories close down for various reasons, throwing people out of work, and as products change and market forces operate firms are forced to convert their products to keep pace. Defence in this regard is just another product. In terms of political attitudes it is noticeable that politicians who oppose defence cutbacks on the grounds that unemployment will rise are frequently members of governments who seem entirely indifferent towards the rise of unemployment in non-defence industries.

Although useful, the policy of attracting new firms to areas has two drawbacks. First, it is expensive and the record of activity over the past 20 years indicates that it is a very cumbersome way of creating employment. Second, it is still to some extent wasteful of the existing infrastructure, although in this case it is not so much the social amenities of the community as the original factories themselves. The most sensible policy is to find ways in which existing firms can convert from defence to civilian production while operating from their existing premises and whenever possible using the same or similar machinery. This strategy has the advantages of minimizing the costs of new plant and equipment, avoiding the duplication of facilities and enabling the workforce to use their existing skills.

Not all processes will be even partly adaptable in this way. A small number will have drawbacks in terms of the remoteness of their location, the toxic nature of the products they formerly processed or the absolute specialization of their defence output, which mean that no conversion is possible.[22] In the vast majority of cases, however, conversion will be an option alongside the attraction of new industries. The actual conversion plans themselves cannot be determined at national level, but only the broad strategy of conversion. The details of what new products to produce, how best to achieve the changeover and so on would be a matter for planning at the local level. The outcome would depend on many factors, including amongst others the equipment available, the local resource and skills base, design traditions and the state of the market in various possible products. These conditions would be so localized that it would not even be possible to standardize conversion plans for a particular industry.[23] The goal would be to convert in a manner which minimizes the need for acquiring new equipment or for major changes in the numbers or training of the workforce.[24]

In the US, national and local government has been alert to this problem for many years. The Department of Defence has an Office of Economic Adjustment (OEA) specifically designed to help communities to overcome difficulties associated with defence cutbacks affecting the local area. So successful has the OEA been that in the overwhelming majority of cases it has been able to create more new jobs in the area than were lost as a result of defence closures.[25] A 1968 study by the government of California, which identified 127 basic occupations involved in defence engineering, found that all but six of these had an obvious civilian counterpart occupation and workers in the remaining six would need six months' retraining to adapt their specialist skills to a non-military occupation.[26]

In the case of management of firms, it is not so much new skills which are required as new attitudes. The economic environment in which the managers of defence firms operate is quite different from that of their counterparts in civilian production. In civil firms, to make profits it is necessary to produce good quality, desirable products at prices the consumer can afford. This is not the case with defence firms. They operate on a cost-plus basis: the consumer (government) pays the cost of development plus a guaranteed profit. There is therefore no incentive to keep the cost of production down; quite the reverse. Where there is only one supplier quality control may not matter too much either. A firm operating on these premises in the civil market will go out of business very quickly. It has been estimated that to retrain and reorient management for the different environment of the civilian market would take up to 18 months.[27]

The success or otherwise of such programmes will depend on the attitude of central government and on the performance of the economy as a whole. Retraining programmes are expensive and in the past have met resistance from those they were designed to help. One key factor is that workers are more likely to embrace retraining schemes if they feel that at the end of the exercise their new skills will gain them employment. This is more likely if the labour market is fairly buoyant. Central government can help, therefore, both in making retraining possible in the locality and in pursuing expansionary macro-economic policies. Extra funding has to be directed towards areas of particular defence reliance because government economic stimulants have an across-the-board effect on the economy as a whole and need to be supplemented in the area of greatest need.

The historical record suggests that the type of macro-economic stimulant chosen is also important. The recession during the Eisenhower years was caused by the decision to cut defence spending at a time when non-defence spending was also being cut. The only boost given to aggregate demand was in the form of tax cuts. However, not only were these cuts too limited – they affected only a very small proportion of the well-off – but tax cuts are an inefficient economic stimulant. Tax reductions generate less economic activity than is lost by equivalent cuts in public spending because of the effects of the 'balanced budget multiplier'. If tax cuts are to be used as an economic stimulant, therefore, the tax cuts must be markedly greater than the reductions in government spending. [28]

The evidence thus suggests that significant reductions in military spending will have no significant detrimental affects on the economy, as long as the reductions have been anticipated by the government and measures have been put in hand to stimulate an offsetting rise in aggregate demand, to transfer economic resources to areas most affected by military cutbacks and to facilitate the conversion of defence to civilian production.

Does Defence Spending Help or Hurt the Economy?

The economic impact of a major defence effort needs to be looked at also in terms of economic growth. If high defence spending hurts the economy then, irrespective of short-term effects, the economy will benefit over the longterm from a transfer of resources to the civilian sector. If defence spending is an economic gain, then further economic offsets to compensate for its loss will be required.

Some economists have seen a positive gain for the economy in defence spending. A 1972 study, for example, found that there was a positive correlation between increases in defence expenditure and increased economic growth rates for 44 developing countries for the period 1950–65.[29] A 1982 UN report acknowledged the correlation but disagreed with the implications, arguing that 'the causality was probably reversed, that is, higher military spending was made possible due to high rates of growth, and not vice-versa.'[30]

Studies of both East and West have produced similar evidence, however, indicating that in some Western states there has been a positive relationship between the defence share of GDP and growth in manufacturing productivity,[31] and that for the NATO and WTO states the opportunity costs of defence exist, but are not particularly significant.[32] One way in which defence might boost the economy was suggested by Merrill Lynch, a firm of American economists, whose model of the US economy indicated that an initial injection of defence spending boosted growth by 40 per cent more than a similar injection of non-defence spending would have done over a six-year period.[33] Stephen Russell has summarized this positive view of the economic effect of defence spending, arguing that 'defense spending initiatives tend to create jobs if there is slack in the economy, and push the state of technology in the pure and applied forms. The "spin-off" of defence-related technology is also a very positive side-effect.'[34]

The majority of economists do not share this view, however, and tend to believe that defence spending has a negative impact on 'investment, inflation, employment, balance of payments, industrial productivity and economic growth'.[35] Some have described the economic effect of defence as 'overwhelmingly negative'[36] and there is a general consensus that the transfer of defence resources to other areas of the economy would stimulate investment and increase economic growth.[37]

The basis of this consensus lies in the evidence that military spending has a profound impact upon the R and D base of developed economies. In his Farewell Address in 1961, President Eisenhower warned the nation that 'the Military Establishment, not productive of itself, necessarily must feed on the energy, productivity and brainpower of the country, and if it takes too much, our total strength declines.' Four years earlier the *Economist* had noted that the real cost of the British defence effort 'is not the 10 per cent that it takes of the national income. It is the 60 per cent that defence pre-empts of all the resources this country can assemble to invest in technological progress.'[38]

It has been a matter of empirical observation for many years that the two Western states with the strongest economies, West Germany and Japan, were two states who made a comparatively small defence effort in proportion to their GNP. The key variable at work seems to have been that of research. It was not so much that total spending on defence was low, but rather that spending on military R and D was low and research on civilian products correspondingly high. It seems to be more than a coincidence that the two Western states with the highest defence R and D effort, Britain and the US, have the lowest growth rates. The two with the lowest defence R and D, West Germany and Japan, have the highest growth rates.

The defence R and D effort is essentially parasitical, feeding off private industry and in particular taking the most talented researchers and absorbing the productive efforts of the hi-tech firms. The high and guaranteed profits which firms can make in the defence field has already been noted, as these form a temptation which many hi-tech firms find compelling. Compared to the cosy world of defence contracting the civilian market is a ruthless jungle to be avoided. Paradoxically, however, it is only the wealth created by firms operating in the civilian market which can produce the resources for governments to maintain high defence outlays and thereby sustain the defence firms.

In 1980, 54 per cent of Britain's publicly funded R and D went to defence, compared with 47 per cent in the US, 35 per cent in France and only 10 per cent in West Germany.[39] Profits in defence-oriented British firms increased by 5.2 per cent on average in 1982 compared with 1.2 per cent for firms in civilian industries.[40] The US appeared to be avoiding President Eisenhower's dire prophecy for many years, because increases in defence spending tended to take funds from consumption rather than investment, while defence cuts also fell on consumption. In the 1980s, however, the correlation seems to have become marked. In the first two years of the Reagan presidency defence R and D spending doubled to $31 billion while civilian R and D fell by $3 billion to $14 billion.[41]

Neither does the 'spin-off' argument have a great deal to commend it. Spin-offs there undoubtedly are. Radar, jet aircraft, satellites, atomic energy and many other advances have originated in defence requirements before becoming generally available through civil adaptations. Even anti-depressant drugs have been produced from components of ballistic missile fuels: a useful by-product to give to the people upset by the prospects of the missiles ever being fired!

The spin-off argument makes little sense, however: 'it is difficult to see how directing attention to one area of technical research would routinely produce an *efficient* generation of knowledge pertaining to a completely different area',[42] or, as Bruce Russett put it, 'the odds are better that a new treatment for cancer will come from medical research than from work on missile systems.'[43]

The point is that while military research does have useful effects on the civilian economy it is simply not as useful in this regard as direct investment in civil R and D would be, as the Japanese experience has clearly demonstrated. Resources released from defence research could therefore be expected to have a direct benefit to a state's wealth-creating potential.

The Impact on Soviet-Style Economies

Superpower arms reductions would have economic impacts on both sides of the Iron Curtain, but the economic systems of East and West differ significantly. Moreover, it is frequently argued in the West that it is the Soviet Union's economic problems which have disposed her to seek negotiated arms reductions in the first place. While the notion of Soviet economic frailty is greatly exaggerated, it is worth looking at how the Communist economic systems differ from those in the West in terms of the economic effects of defence and disarmament.

Although Soviet leaders do not like to emphasize the heavy burden of defence spending, under Mr Gorbachev they have been more willing to admit that the Soviet economy would benefit from the freeing of resources currently tied up in defence production or research.[44] Moreover, Soviet commentators have hinted at this obliquely for many years by describing the benefits the capitalist and developing worlds would gain from disarmament. One Soviet writer spoke of increased international trade and levels of foreign aid which would make it possible to 'irrigate the Sahara and other deserts, to turn them into flowering fields and gardens'.[45] Allowing for the hyperbole which is common among Russian authors, it is nevertheless possible to imagine the hopes the Soviets must have of irrigating their own southern territories if only the enormous funds and technical resources required could be released.

For many years Soviet commentators tended to cite militarization as the main reason for economic problems in the West, equating military production with waste. It was also argued that high defence spending was deliberately pursued in the West in order to overcome the inevitable dislocations of the cyclical nature of capitalist production.[46] In the 1970s a more fractured analysis emerged, with some Soviet writers continuing to insist that the arms race benefited Western industrialists, and others arguing that arms spending damaged Western economies.[47] In practice, as noted earlier, both analyses have some truth. Defence spending does hurt Western economies, but defence firms benefit from the funding denied to their civil counterparts. The same phenomenon, however, appeared to be at work in the Soviet Union during the 1960s and 1970s, where the massive Soviet military build-up was accompanied by a decline in the Soviet Union's economic growth rate.[48]

The problems created for the Soviet economy by the defence burden are different in important respects from those imposed on the free market economies of the West. This is because of the differences in the way the Soviet economy operates.

The economies of the Communist states are 'command economies'. Decisions relating to the allocation of productive resources are determined by a centralized political and economic leadership rather than being the result of the interaction of supply and demand with the profit-seeking motivations of entrepreneurs as is the case in the West. In Communist economies everything comes down to planning, and resource allocation is done in terms of priorities. The nature of the political system means that the 'consumer' is the state, which is also the producer, so the leadership's assumptions about what needs are vital are the sole criteria for production.

In practice this means that all industries are ranked in order of priority. The higher that industry's priority the greater the resources available, in terms of supplies, manpower and scientific skills. In the Soviet Union the defence sector sits at the top of every queue for resources. This has the effect, therefore, of denying resources to the civilian sector in very much the same way as happens in the capitalist states. As in the West, the Soviet system 'in effect shrinks the resource base of the entire civilian economy'.[49]

However, if defence exertions place similar burdens on the Soviet and Western economies, the problems inherent in moving away from defence to civilian production ought to be easier to cope with for the command economies than for free market ones. The solution to these problems lies in planning and government intervention rather than in the operation of unguided market forces, and clearly a command economy is better placed to implement such direction since it sees this as the norm. Soviet specialists have argued for some time that this is the case.[50]

Although their centralized planning apparatus would ease the problems of conversion to civilian production, Soviet-style economies would still face difficulties in this regard. As noted earlier, conversion programmes would need to be planned at a very devolved level and the highly centralized nature of Communist states might cause a rather inflexible blueprint for all factories to be laid down which failed to take into account the particular local circumstances relevant in each case.

Soviet managers would also probably find it as difficult to adjust as their Western counterparts. They, too, are used to producing high performance equipment without any overriding concern as to how much the final product costs. While Western managers would have difficulty coping with the cost disciplines of the civilian market, Soviet managers would struggle without the easy access to high-quality resources to which they had been used in the defence sector. It has also been suggested that they might feel a loss of status in moving from defence to civil production, although this might be offset by the greater acclaim for achievement possible in a less secretive career.[51] Overall, therefore, although not without its own difficulties, the conversion process for socialist economies should be slightly easier than for market economies, while the benefits to be gained would be just as great.

The Economics of Arms Control

As noted in chapter 1, arms control may involve reductions but does not necessarily do so. The discussion so far in this chapter has been based upon the likely economic impact of arms control agreements which led to significant reductions in manpower or weaponry.

Arms control which involves reductions – that is, disarmament – produces reasonably straightforward either/or results. If disarmament occurs, defence spending will fall and this will have certain predictable results. If no disarmament occurs, defence spending will stay the same or rise and this too will produce economic effects. In practice, however, arms control has manifested itself over the past two decades in ways which make these either/or calculations too simplistic. In some cases arms control agreements have legitimized increases, rather than reductions, in armaments. In these cases the argument has been about whether even more weapons than the totals agreed upon would have been acquired in the absence of the agreement, and therefore what the additional costs would have been. In other cases arms control agreements have reduced competition in some areas, but had a consequential effect of stimulating military competition in other, unconstrained areas, in which case the costs/savings calculus becomes far more complicated. Both these phenomena raise the question of whether arms control really does save money, as its original proponents assumed it would.[52]

During the debate in the US over the merits of the SALT I agreement in the early 1970s, President Nixon's administration argued that in the absence of SALT I the US would need to spend an additional $15–20 billion in order to maintain its security at the same level that SALT I gave.[53] Senator Henry Jackson rather unkindly called this claim 'nonsense on stilts'.[54] During the SALT II debates Secretary of Defense Harold Brown again extolled the budgetary virtues of the treaty, claiming that it would produce a saving of $2 billion per year on defence spending.

The claims made for the SALT agreements by the Nixon and Carter administrations were based upon two logical arguments. In the first place there were some direct savings involved in the fact that certain weapon systems were constrained. Thus, for example, after

1974 the US was not allowed to build more than one ABM base and therefore 'saved' money she might have spent on additional sites (in fact the US did not even bother with the one site permitted her under the treaty). Second, since the USSR was similarly constrained, the US saved money that would have had to have been spent on systems designed to penetrate an unconstrained Soviet ABM defence.

Advocates of SALT argued that it reduced the need for worst-case assumptions. The upper limits on weapons allowed, together with restrictions on new programmes, meant that you have a much better idea of what the other side has, and what they would have in a decade to come. Moreover, the verification clauses meant that you could check up on the other side so that your 'guesstimates' were more accurate. The result of all this would be that you would need to acquire fewer weapons to match the other side: *ergo* you would save money.

However, it is extraordinarily difficult to be sure of how much you 'might' have spent and therefore how much has been theoretically 'saved'. The US government estimated that SALT I saved some $11 billion over the period 1973–81, but these figures were for cost-avoidance rather than for savings. SALT I has not led to direct savings.[55] Similarly, Harold Brown argued only that SALT II would reduce the scale of the increase in defence spending, not that it would reduce such spending. Without SALT he argued a 60 per cent increase was required; with SALT a 25 per cent increase would be sufficient.[56]

However, an arms control agreement may entail certain additional costs. In order to ease verification problems for the Soviet Union while increasing the survivability of the US ICBM force, President Carter proposed deploying the MX missile in a basing mode that was enormously expensive. One critic of SALT II actually claimed that SALT would *add* up to $12 billion to the defence budget rather than save money.[57]

More significantly, there are real costs imposed upon arms control outcomes by the domestic bargaining process which accompanies arms control negotiations. There is a tendency for agreements to be accompanied by assurances to certain vested interests that they will not suffer as a result of the negotiated defence constraints. Service chiefs have to be bought off with new weapons programmes; legislators with defence establishments in their constituencies have to be assured that defence contracts for new weapons still come to make up for those no longer being produced; legislators unhappy with the treaty must be reassured with a vigorous military build-up in areas not covered by the agreement. All this means more weapons and more spending.

The SALT I agreement was therefore followed by a $1 billion increase in funds allocated to the Trident and B-1 bomber programmes. The SALT II debate saw a number of senators declaring that they would only vote for the treaty if it were accompanied by a significant increase in the defence budget.[58] This pressure was so great that an increase in spending of $100 billion over the following ten years was forecast, over and above projected increases.[59] Some liberal senators indicated that they felt that these costs were so great as to make the treaty a loss rather than a gain for arms control and therefore they would vote against it.[60] The overall impression confirmed the suspicions of one of the early writers on arms control, Kenneth Boulding, who in 1961 had noted that 'there are those who argue that arms control might lead to a larger military budget, especially if control were confined to the weapons of mass destruction.'[61]

Conclusions

An examination of the economic effects of arms control and disarmament is important both because in the minds of many disarmament is associated with economic recession[62] and because the saving of money was one of the goals sought through arms control by its original proponents.[63] It is important, therefore, to determine its realistic likely effects under varying conditions and to eliminate unnecessary concerns. In this regard the evidence seems to consist of some good news and some bad news.

The good news is that disarmament – that is, arms control involving reductions – will not generate major economic difficulties so long as the necessary planning and implementation of the correct macro-economic policy is carried out. Disarmament need not lead to recession.

The bad news is that disarmament and arms control are not likely to save much, if any, money. In the case of disarmament, in order to maintain aggregate demand and prevent recession money will have to be poured into civilian spending as it is released by defence cuts. People will gain more tangible benefits from their taxes, but those taxes will be just as high as before. In the longer term stimulation of the civilian economy may generate wealth which will raise living standards while reducing taxation levels, but this can only be a long-term, not a short-term, goal.

In the case of arms control the economic benefits are even less tangible. Arms control to date has helped to stabilize the global balance of power, but it has not saved money and neither, given the domestic politics of arms control negotiations (discussed in chapter 5), does there seem much chance that it can do so. To the extent that competition is channelled from nuclear to conventional weapons, the expense will if anything be even greater.

In the final analysis, however, an important point must not be lost sight of. It is relevant to note that disarmament will not lead to economic disaster, but arms control is about security and survival, and the continuation of both is something for which, logically, no price is too high. If security and economy can go hand in hand this is all to the good but, when economic and security needs conflict, if the money can be found, it must be found. Similarly, when arms control offers the best route to security, then it remains the best route even if it is a more expensive route, because at the end of the day the costs of nuclear war are incalculable.

5

Talking to Yourself:
Domestic Arms Control
Bargaining

We dissipate energies negotiating with ourselves.

Newhouse, *Cold Dawn: The Story of SALT*[1]

The promise of arms control as an instrument of national security policy has been stunted as much by domestic political factors as by any other.

Miller, 'Politics over Promise: The Domestic Impediments to Arms Control[2]

Introduction

Modern international arms control is a process involving two sets of parallel negotiations which are both crucial to the outcome of attempts by states to enter into arms control security relationships. On the one hand, there are the bilateral or multilateral negotiations between the states themselves, such as the SALT talks or the negotiations for the NPT. On the other hand, there is the debate and bargaining within states both as to the negotiating strategy and tactics to be employed at the international talks and that relating to the domestic wheeling and dealing which is required in order to produce a majority behind the eventual agreement. It is not always obvious that the international aspect is the more important of the two.

The domestic debate influences the progress and even the possibility of arms control in a number of ways. When arms control talks with another state are under way there will be many domestic political opponents of the negotiations. These will have to be appeased in various ways. Some will only accept restraints in one area of defence procurement if other areas have more funds allotted to them. Some will want particular weapons protected because they happen to be manufactured in that particular politician's constituency. Some may demand the adoption of new domestic or foreign policy initiatives in return for their vote for the arms control agreement. Some may want changes in a particular aspect of the treaty. Others may expect future political favours as the price of their support.

The end result of all this manoeuvring is that the shape and content of the eventual agreement, the international environment in which it is born, the manner in which it is implemented, the spirit in which it is (or is not) adhered to and a host of other factors crucial to the eventual value and effectiveness of an arms control agreement, will be affected by domestic political bargaining rather than the impact of international bargaining.

Internal Bargaining

Negotiating with an adversary is always a tortuous and difficult business, but those difficulties are dramatically compounded when the real aim of the negotiations for a state differs from its publicly stated objectives or when, in fact, that government has no real idea what its real goals actually are. This problem has plagued the bilateral negotiations between the superpowers because for much of the past 20 years the US has lacked a consistent set of negotiating objectives.[3] The political dynamics of superpower relations tend to drive the two states towards arms control negotiations, but the complexity of international security relationships means that negotiations may begin at a time when one or both parties is not at all clear what exactly it wants from the negotiations. Arms control offers are then stitched together for political purposes and these offers may have immense strategic implications and yet may not have been properly thought through. They are the result of the interplay of domestic political forces and manoeuvring among various sections of the government, rather than being a coherent response to clearly perceived strategic goals. An American participant in the SALT negotiations noted that the continuous struggles between various sectors of the US foreign policy establishment over the detail of the negotiations tended to undermine the chances of the US being able to pursue a consistent and effective strategy in its bargaining with the Soviet Union.[4] Indeed President Carter ruefully remarked in his memoirs that SALT II required as much negotiation in the US as it did with the Soviet Union.[5]

The US is particularly hamstrung in this respect because its very constitution seems to be designed to maximize the possibilities for confusion and disharmony within the policy-making process. A notable feature of the constitution is that: 'In a Congress of 535 members, 33 Senators plus one can block a treaty.'[6] This modern US version of the *liberum veto* means that groups within and outside the government know that they only need to plant the seeds of doubt in the minds of 34 people to prevent an agreement from being ratified. The mere suspicion that it lacks those 34 votes usually dissuades an administration from putting the matter to the test. President John F. Kennedy, for example, wanted to sign a comprehensive nulcear test ban in 1963 but he feared that the Senate would not ratify such an agreement and therefore signed a limited test ban instead.[7] Similar doubts about the TTBT, the PNET and the SALT II Treaty led Presidents Nixon, Ford and Carter to withhold putting them to a Senate vote.

The executive branch's fear of public rejection of a treaty negotiated in good faith has placed the US in the position of having ratified almost none of the arms control treaties it has signed with the Soviet Union: a position it would doubtless find to be intolerable and clear evidence of Soviet duplicity were the positions to be reversed. Moreover, the requirements of states relating to treaties which they have signed but not yet ratified are governed by the 1969 Vienna Convention on the Law of Treaties. The US, it almost goes without saying, has signed the Vienna Convention, but has not as yet ratified it![8]

The constitution of the US exerts a baleful influence on arms control in other ways as well. One clear determinant of arms control policy in the US is the electoral cycle. Presidential elections occur every four years and elections for the whole of the House of Representatives and one-third of the Senate occur every two years. Impending elections concentrate the mind of an administration wonderfully and there have been several occasions when an administration has shifted gear sharply as elections approached and rushed forward a series of arms control proposals in an attempt to achieve a breakthrough before election day. President Nixon did this with the

SALT I agreements signed in May 1972 prior to the presidential
election campaign, and President Reagan did it with the Reykjavik
proposals of October 1986 prior to crucial mid-term elections. In both
cases the result was a hastily contrived hodgepodge worthy in intent
but full of ambiguity and clearly containing vast scope for subsequent
confusion and argument. On the other hand, when they have feared
an acrimonious debate on the proposals governments have also post-
poned completion or submission of worthy agreements in the hope
that they can be easily dealt with after a successful campaign for re-
election. Under the pressure of Ronald Reagan's bitter anti-arms
control campaigns both President Ford in 1976 and President Carter
in 1980 placed a SALT II agreement in a limbo from which their
subsequent electoral defeats left them unable to retrieve it.

The fact that the US is nowadays engaged in a more-or-less continuous election campaign, together with the fact that a limited
number of legislators have tremendous power makes it extraordinarily difficult to push arms control through the system. The manner
in which arms control was conducted after 1969 – that is, the pursuit
of unwieldy catch-all agreements – only made matters worse since the
overall agreement was held hostage to the doubts of a few senators
about one or two of any agreement's innumerable clauses. To get
around this latter problem it has been suggested that administrations
should seek to push forward numbers of limited agreements rather
than try to cover everything in a single treaty. This would mean both
that some arms control would actually be occurring as the less contentious agreements were acted upon, and that if the Senate chose to
block or reject a proposal it would matter less if it were only a limited,
discrete agreement.[9]

One obvious way to produce a more coherent and rational
direction of arms control policy would be to limit the number of
bureaucratic actors involved in its formulation. Unfortunately this is
far easier said than done. For one thing many institutions have a
powerful vested interest in structuring issues so as to make their
involvement necessary. Thus, for example, a new weapon system is
essentially a military issue, something for the Pentagon to be
concerned with. Once the implications of the weapon make it an arms
control issue, however, other bodies such as The Arms Control and
Disarmament Agency ACDA and the State Department have a legitimate interest. The more weapons that are actual or potential arms

control issues the more influence the State Department has on defence and national security policy. Conversely, the Pentagon has an institutional political reason for wishing to minimize arms control issues in order to limit State Department interference in what it considers its own territory.

However, some sympathizers with Pentagon attitudes argue from a different perspective that while weapons should be allowed to become arms control issues, the Pentagon must then have the dominant influence over arms control policy. Richard Burt, for example, has argued that the creation of ACDA was a mistake and that the Joint Chiefs of Staff and 'senior elements' of the US armed forces should be given a far more central role both in arms control planning and in the conduct of the actual negotiations.[10]

ACDA, in fact, has always been controversial. Although it might be thought reasonable to give the arms control agency a central role in arms control policy this is something it has never had. On the contrary, for much of its history it has been held in deep suspicion by the executive and by Congress, largely because of a feeling that it is actually in favour of genuine arms control. Henry Kissinger called ACDA's officials 'arms controllers', a phrase which for him represented the ultimate insult[11], while one congressional critic suggested that by carrying out research into arms control policy implications ACDA was 'studying reasons for the free world to surrender to the Kremlin'.[12] It is hardly surprising that critics of this persuasion feel that arms control, if it is to be bothered with at all, should be left in the hands of the Pentagon. Sceptics might feel that this is analagous to placing responsibility for the eventual abolition of all violins in the hands of Yehudi Menuhin.

The deference shown to the uniformed military on arms control issues is largely a function of the time pressures acting upon legislators. Members of Congress, for example, have too little time to make themselves expert on every issue that might come before them, but on domestic issues such as health, education or law and order they are apt to feel that their opinion is as good as anyone's. On defence and foreign policy, however, they are far more likely to feel inhibited by the complexity of the issues and the technologies involved and will therefore defer to the experts. In the words of Congressman Les Aspin: 'to most Congressmen defence experts are people in uniform, not academics in universities or "think tanks".

Uniforms equal expertise, and the higher the rank, the greater the expert.'[13]

There is in addition a tendency to view the military as 'safe' on arms control. It is a political fact that to a certain extent conservative leaders can deliver arms control in a way that liberals find difficult because, to those sceptical of arms control, a conservative leader can be trusted not to 'give away the store'. President Nixon's arms control initiatives won greater domestic support than President Carter's because Nixon was seen as a hawk who would not have made dangerous concessions to the Soviet Union, whereas Carter's image aroused suspicion among conservative Americans.

Even President Nixon, whose foreign policy achievements (especially in arms control) will probably (and deservedly) eventually eclipse his domestic failings in the historical record, felt a suspicion of ACDA and the arms control 'establishment'. Like Kissinger he suspected committed arms controllers of a 'vague disloyalty' to his administration.[14] Some congressional leaders, such as the influential Senator Henry Jackson, had an even lower opinion of ACDA officials.[15] Jackson's dislike of arms controllers extended to those who had been responsible for the SALT I agreement, and at his urging a purge of arms control staff took place in 1972 in order to produce a SALT 2 negotiating team which had minimal overlap with those who had negotiated SALT 1.[16] The purge may have kept Senator Jackson happy for a brief period, but it did not help with continuity in policy formulation.

Domestic Politics

Domestic politics has a profound impact upon the pursuit of arms control. A crucial determinant is the attitude of public opinion. Professional politicians tend to be single-minded individuals and their great aim in life is to remain in office. All other considerations pale into insignificance beside this. The product of their labours – that is, the formulation and implementation of policy – is something 'of secondary importance, relevant only to the extent that it contributes to the success of the professionals'.[17] Politicians therefore will follow their inclination on arms control to the extent that they think the general public will approve of their actions. The nature of public attitudes towards arms control in the US is consequently crucial.

In practice ordinary US citizens are ambivalent towards arms control. On the one hand, they are generally supportive of the idea, believing that states should seek to achieve greater mutual security by negotiation. On the other hand, when it comes down to specific agreements with the Soviet Union the same public may withhold its support. In the final analysis they would prefer (as any people would) military superiority over a potential adversary to mere equality, since they trust their government not to misuse that superiority. In addition there is an anti-arms control body of opinion which can be mobilized to oppose specific treaties. [18]

From the standpoint of a practical politician in the US, therefore, the public's attitude toward arms control is somewhat inconsistent. Certainly the public expects a fairly consistent effort to achieve arms control but it does not expect its representatives to support each and every agreement. It is also vulnerable to manipulation by a determined administration as the rapid turnaround in public attitudes towards the outcome of the Reykjavik summit meeting in October 1986 showed.

This public ambivalence causes US politicians to adopt curious postures at election time. At the time of the SALT II ratification arguments in the summer of 1979 a number of politicians known for their previous support for the SALT process began to display distinct hostility towards the SALT II treaty. Senator Frank Church of Idaho, for example, a noted liberal on arms control isues, launched a series of attacks on alleged Soviet untrustworthiness which was bound to increase opposition to the treaty. He took this stance because he faced a difficult Senate re-election campaign in 1980 in a conservative state against a hawkish Republican opponent. Church felt compelled to adopt this conservative political stance as the election approached because the opinion polls showed him to be in real danger of losing his seat. In the event he lost anyway.

Another politician who took a similarly surprising anti-SALT attitude in 1980 was Senator Howard Baker of Tennessee. Baker's problem was not quite the same as Church's. Baker was one of the many Republicans hoping for his party's nomination for the 1980 presidential election. In 1977 Baker, a liberal Republican, had angered his party's right wing by supporting President Carter on the issue of the Panama Canal Treaty, which set out a timetable for the eventual attainment of Panamanian sovereignty over the Canal. The

Panama debate was a fiercely contested political issue in the US and the Carter administration lobbied very hard to gain a narrow majority for ratification of the treaty. Several senators indicated as early as 1978 that they felt President Carter had used up his political favours in the Senate and that SALT II would therefore be in for a rougher ride than would have been the case if the Panama Canal issue had not been so contentious.[19] For Senator Baker this was particularly true and he felt that having supported President Carter on one devisive issue in 1977 he could not do so again in 1979 if he was to have any chance of gaining the Republican presidential nomination. He therefore announced that he would oppose SALT II even though it was known that he privately hoped the treaty would pass anyway.

Domestic politics in 1980 meant that arguments over SALT II only rarely related to the substance of the treaty. Far more often they were tangential issues relevant only in so far as the political environment had made them so. Thus, for example, the Panama Canal Treaties as such had nothing to do with SALT II, but when the American Conservative Union attacked the Panama treaties as 'a policy of abject surrender and symptomatic of a national retreat',[20] this affected the tone of the subsequent SALT II debate as members of Congress sought to display firmess on foreign policy and shied away from anything that would make them vulnerable to conservative attacks.

Although members of Congress are generally less assertive on foreign policy issues than on domestic policy, Congress does sometimes exert itself. Indeed, it has on occasion shown a greater awareness of the arms control implications of certain weapon systems than the executive branch. In the late 1960s, for example, a number of Senators tried to bring to the administration's attention the problems that would be caused for the US if both superpowers went ahead and deployed MIRV nuclear warheads on their missiles. On 17 June 1969, Senator Edward Brooke introduced Senate Resolution 211 which called on the President to work for a superpower moratorium on MIRV flight-testing.[21] There is nowadays a consensus that the failure to ban MIRVs was a catastrophic misjudgement by the US which created many of the strategic difficulties in which it now finds itself. President Nixon's response to the Brooke Resolution at the time, however, was simple: 'I think the Resolution really is irrelevant to what we are going to do.'[22]

Similarly, on 25 February 1976 a group of senators led by Edward Kennedy introduced Resolution 399 which called for a superpower moratorium on the flight-testing of strategic cruise missiles.[23] The executive ignored this also and in the long run this failure will probably come to haunt NATO for the same sort of reasons as the MIRV misjudgement: in the end Soviet reciprocation will produce an increased threat to the West. More recently Congress has taken the lead in trying to impose a moratorium on the testing of ASAT weapons[24] and again it is Congress rather than the Executive branch which has shown the clearer grasp of the long-term security interests of the West. These examples do show, however, that even when Congress is active, and is correct on the issue, it may still be unable to influence events significantly. Only in the ASAT case was it able to enforce a limitation on the nature of the weapons tests being carried out, and even then it proved unable to end testing completely.

Linkage

As noted earlier, one of the complexities thrown up by the interaction of domestic and international politics is the linkage of arms control with peripheral issues for political purposes. It has long been argued by members of the arms control community that arms control is too important to be linked with general foreign policy issues and that ways should be found to isolate it from the ups and downs of East–West relationships. However laudable in theory, this goal is impossible to achieve in practice. While it is possible for governments to refrain from directly linking progress in arms control to progress in other areas, it is not possible to prevent people's perceptions from making this kind of linkage. Public opinion in the US, outraged by Soviet actions in Afghanistan, is less likely to support the conclusion of superpower nuclear arms deals even though events in Afghanistan have no direct connection with warhead totals in the US. Both superpowers have stressed linkage whenever they felt it to be in their interest to do so, and opposed it on other occasions.

Generally speaking the Soviet Union has not attached much importance to linking arms control to more general policy issues. For example, at the time of the signing of the SALT I agreement, the US stepped up its bombing of North Vietnam and mined the harbour of Haiphong which was much used by Soviet shipping. The Soviets did not allow this to interfere with the SALT I agreements, however. The Soviet Union has linked differing arms control issues though: for example, at times trying progress on an INF deal in Europe to the satisfactory conclusion of an agreement on strategic defences with the US.[25]

The US, in contrast, has consistently used linkage in an attempt to influence the Soviet Union, particularly on human rights issues. Linkage has taken 'firm root in the American political system and, as a result, imposed a heavier burden on the talks than they could possibly bear'.[26] Arms control negotiations are sufficiently complex in their own right and, for a variety of reasons discussed in this book, have enough difficulty in resolving security problems between states without expecting them to unlock foreign emigration quotas, empty Soviet prisons or resolve equally complex problems in other issue areas.

The very logic of linkage is open to doubt. It rests on the assumption that the other side needs the arms control agreement more than you do. In the past, however, treaties have come when both superpowers have agreed that they gain more than they lose by signing the treaty. No agreements have been signed in circumstances in which either side gave the impression that it had to have an agreement at any cost and could not contemplate failure to achieve one. Even with SALT I, where there were strong economic incentives to agree, the USSR 'strenuously rejected the idea of linkage or the implicit assumption that they wanted or needed a SALT agreement more than did the United States'.[27]

The real problem with linkage is the unavoidable resonance of global political conflicts within the US domestic political environment. Frustrations with Soviet behaviour worldwide are inevitable given the differing value system and global interests of the two sides. Because their interests *are* global there is virtually always at least one issue or area of the world where friction between the superpowers is marked at any one time. It is therefore impossible to insulate arms control from these vagaries. The idea that arms control is too important to allow it to be affected in this way is a non-starter. It is affected because the overall superpower relationship at any one time will 'define the realm of the possible in American politics'[28] with regard to foreign policy and arms control.

If such an insulation could be achieved, it would be a tremendous gain. Linkage of arms control progress with Soviet behaviour 'is the

most frequently remarked upon impediment to successful negotiation'.[29] Even without wishing it, linkage can appear to block
progress, however. There is no doubt that the 1978 decision by the
US finally to accord full diplomatic recognition to the People's
Republic of China angered the Soviet Union and slowed down the
SALT II negotiations. Overall, therefore, linkage is inevitable and is
a factor which obstructs progress in arms control; in terms of practi-
calities the most that can be done to minimize its effects is to refrain
from deliberate fostering of linkages by governments for political
ends.

Displacement Effects

Arms control agreements to date have had no appreciable impact in
terms of restraining the growth of defence budgets. If anything the
reverse is true, and the success rate of Congress in restraining defence
outlays caused it to be compared unfavourably as a government
watchdog to the Tudor parliaments of Henry VIII.[30] One of the
reasons for this is the 'displacement effect' of arms control negotiations. When an agreement places restraints on weapons acquisition
or development in one area there is a tendency for the military effort
and expenditure to be simply displaced into another area. In many
cases in fact the overall level of spending tends to increase, rather
than decrease, after an arms control agreement. In the words of one
of the US negotiators of SALT I: 'when some things are proscribed,
energies and interests tend to flow into permitted areas.'[31]

Sometimes the scale of this diverted effort may be so great as to
raise doubts as to whether the arms control treaty represents a
genuine gain. At the time of the SALT II debates, for example,
Senator Sam Nunn of Georgia, an influential defence specialist,
declared that he would only vote for the treaty if it were accompanied
by a major increase in the defence budget. Senator Howard
Metzenbaum of Ohio said he would prefer no SALT treaty at all to
one 'whose ratification will require the diversion to military spending
of billions of dollars that could better be used to meet the nation's
urgent human needs'.[32]

A number of points are raised by this issue. One obvious improvement in terms of advancing arms control goals would be to try and
estimate when bargaining is under way, the degree to which arms

control gains in one area outweigh the losses in another and proceed or not, on that basis. Again this is logical, but extremely difficult to achieve in practice because the displacement spending is the result of political horse-trading.

To get arms control agreements through the US legislative mine-field, the approval of the Joint Chiefs of Staff (JCS) is required. Without their favourable testimony regarding the military impact of the agreement Congress is likely to remain sceptical as to whether it is actually in the best interests of the US. As noted earlier Congress tends to see the uniformed military as being the experts in these fields. The Joint Chiefs use this powerful position to extract conces-sions on the development of new weapons programmes in return for their favourable testimony. Thus Henry Kissinger noted that while the JCS were prepared to support SALT I, 'they attached a price tag.'[33] In this particular instance, in return for allowing the USSR a numerical advantage in SSBNs under SALT I, Admiral Moorer was promised the Trident submarine.[34] The Army and Air Force received as their sweeteners a package of programmes including a second ABM site (subsequently revoked) and the B-1 bomber.[35]

The impact of bargaining trade-offs of this sort is so great that it has been suggested that the importance of the military in producing political support for an agreement is such that without explicitly opposing arms control generally, the military are able to limit agree-ments to those which are meaningless in terms of altering the strategic situation or reducing the military budget and that therefore they emasculate arms control without being seen to oppose it.[36] One critic has argued that the ability of the Pentagon to use these tactics has resulted in a serious decline in legislative constraints on defence spending in the past 15 years.[37]

The military in any country are bound to have certain reservations about arms control. These are a product of concern not so much about national security as about job security, though this may not be realized on a conscious level. Professional military officers invariably feel genuinely convinced that reduction in their force's military inventory jeopardizes the nation's safety by weakening their ability to carry out the tasks allotted to them. From their specialist perspective this is a very reasonable point of view. In addition, however, cuts in defence spending inevitably threaten jobs and prestige within military establishments and this is equally important though not normally articulated. Observers of the US military's attitude towards arms control have described it as a distinct 'wariness' largely produced by the fact that 'few officers in the Pentagon have their interests furthered by arms control.'[38]

To keep the military compliant about the restraints imposed by an arms control deal, therefore, their wariness must be overcome by clear gains in other areas. As President Carter noted, the JCS have to be kept happy.[39] As with the problem of linkage, the impact of displacement effects on arms control is something to which attention ought to be paid, but about which it is very difficult to do anything because of the political realities. What can be done, however, is that when arms control and the setting of limited restraints on certain weapons systems are being proposed, consideration should be given as to whether significant displacement spending is likely to occur as a result. The criteria for judging whether the agreement continues to be worth pursuing after the displacement effects are taken into consideration should not be related to cost trade-off but rather whether the overall effect of the package will be to stabilize deterrence.[40] If the effects cancel each other out or if the destabilizing impact of the displacement effects outweigh the stabilization produced by the treaty, then the agreement is not worth proceeding with.

The Effects of Alliance Membership

A further 'domestic' input into a state's arms control posture are the views of its allies. As with domestic public opinion in the US the views of its allies are consistently in favour of the pursuit of arms control as a goal, but do not always extend to support for the position of the US on particular issues. For example, the European NATO allies and Canada fought a determined rearguard action in favour of a 'strict' interpretation of the ABM treaty rather than the 'broad' interpretation favoured by the Reagan administration. The British government, for example, declared that 'we have repeatedly made it clear that we regard the treaty as an important element in preserving international peace and stability and want to see it reaffirmed and strengthened.'[41] In a similar manner the allies pressed the US to remain within the limits established by the SALT II treaty which formally expired at the end of 1985. President Reagan announced in

May 1986 that the US was preparing to withdraw from the treaty.[42] European governments were unanimous in urging him to reconsider and to maintain the agreement. The 'European allies howled', as one observer put it.[43] The administration reacted by backing away from its aggressive statements on SALT II, but eventually deliberately breached a crucial treaty sub-limit in late 1986.

On both SALT I and SALT II the allies have urged the US to maintain its adherence to arm control agreements. On the issue of INF forces in Europe, however, and President Reagan's suggestion of banning all ballistic nuclear missiles, the allies argued that less arms control was required. While the US proposed a zero–zero INF balance in Europe, the European NATO governments would have preferred a balance at a very low level, but one which still maintained some INF on each side.[44] Similarly, European governments would like major reductions in the ballistic missile forces possessed by each side, but not their total abolition. This is because the ballistic missiles are seen as being the most reliable and effective element in the strategic triad which underpins the deterrent retionship: and deterrence is a hallowed concept to European governments who firmly believe that it is a system 'proven by nearly forty years of compulsory peaceful co-existence'.[45]

The NATO allies have been even more confusing in terms of their attitudes towards SDI. The NATO allies are well aware on issues of this sort that there is very little, if anything, they can do if the US is determined to go ahead with a project, so their reservations tend to be coded or uttered behind closed doors. This made the public expressions of deep scepticism about SDI all the more remarkable. The Secretary-General of NATO, the British Foreign Secretary, the French defence minister and the West German Chancellor all publicly expressed their doubts about the strategic wisdom of the project.[46] The European allies feared that if SDI were to work, the US would retreat behind its own defensive shield leaving Europe isolated and vulnerable.[47] Hans-Dietrich Genscher, the West German Foreign Minister, declared that 'we do not want the situation where the superpowers have super security while the lesser powers have lesser security.'[48] A second fear was that, should nuclear defence prove feasible, Europe would face a heightened danger of war. 'Making the world safe for conventional war is not at all appealing for Europeans', in the words of a French Foreign Ministry official.[49]

However, having taken this logical, sensible and coherent view, the European allies steadily muddied the waters over the subsequent two years by their venal pursuit of the financial and technological benefits seen to be achievable by participating in the SDI research programme, despite its being widely recognized that at best Europe would only end up with the technological scraps from the table.[50]

The mixed signals sent by the allies on an issue such as SDI are important. Although the allies have far less real influence over the US administration than they would like, and a great deal less than they pretend, publicly stated allied views are important. This is because of the way in which allied feelings, like other aspects of the external environment, feed in to the US domestic political debate. When Republicans and Democrats are divided on an issue affecting NATO, both will attempt to argue that their own views most closely coincide with the majority view within NATO. The corollary of this is that when the allies appear to support the administration, the opposition feel that their attacks are greatly weakened. Certainly on both the adherence to SALT II and SDI issues, opponents of the Reagan administration policies felt that European views were crucial and could have had a far more determining impact had they been expressed forcefully in public in order to influence the American domestic debate. The problem here is that this is just why the European allies expressed their views in private; they did not want to be seen as breaking ranks with their ally in a way that could be interpreted as interfering in domestic politics. No such restraint affected the US, however, and the Reagan administration cheerfully intervened in a British domestic political debate by denouncing the defence policies of the opposition Labour Party.[51]

Overall, the alliance input seems to have been extremely important since 1980, despite the unwillingness of the allies to rock the boat too much. The Europeans and Canadians pressed consistently for the pursuit of further arms control and for adherence to existing treaties.

Political Leadership

In discussing the domestic bargaining constraints which impose difficulties in the achievement of arms control it is important to make clear that if a president is sufficiently determined, it is possible to overcome many, if not all of these obstacles. One of the most disappointing features of the Reagan presidency was that the administration faced few of the impediments that frequently block progress and yet its record of achievement was so poor. Between 1981 and the beginning of 1987, a period in which he 'enjoyed extraordinary public and congressional support',[52] President Reagan produced nothing to set against the achievements of his predecessors. The absence of will was crucial because 'the strong and direct commitment of the President and his close associates in the White House seems to be a decisive element in determining whether and how much arms control can succeed.'[53] Once domestic setbacks made a foreign policy success essential, President Reagan pushed quickly for the INF treaty of 1987.

A president's commitment will not inevitably bring success. President Carter was able to produce an agreement with the Soviet Union, but was unable to get the SALT II Treaty ratified before he left office, and neither did the many other negotiations carried out during his time in office on issues as diverse as anti-satellite weapons, and conventional arms transfers, produce agreements. Without that commitment, however, no progress is possible because the inevitable bureaucratic impediments will remain in place.

A number of studies have given evidence of the impact the president can have. In the late 1950s the negotiations for a CTB treaty were severely hampered by the fact that President Eisenhower had no strong feelings about the subject. Prior to 1955 those elements in the policy-making bureaucracy who did have strong views were opposed to any ban on continued testing. Not surprisingly, therefore, the US did not push the issue very strongly.[54] In 1955 Eisenhower acquired a new adviser on disarmament issues, Harold Stassen. Stassen favoured a test ban, but because Dulles, the Secretary of State, opposed it the US negotiating position remained deadlocked.[55] Eisenhower did not resolve this situation.

A contrast with the speed possible when the bureaucracy was short-circuited was shown by the events after Stassen resigned. Dulles changed his mind on a CTB and became a proponent. He drafted a letter to Krushchev which was approved by Eisenhower but not shown to Pentagon or Atomic Energy Commission officials. The letter led to the superpower test moratorium shortly afterwards.

A similar effect can be seen with the pathbreaking speech by President John F. Kennedy delivered at American University in Washington in June 1963. The speech, which called for a new pragmatism and generosity of spirit in superpower relations, made a profound impression on the Soviet leadership and in many ways signalled the end of the first 'Cold War'. According to Kennedy's special assistant the speech was drafted by a small group of advisers and 'official departmental positions and suggestions were not solicited.'[56] When Kennedy despatched a team drawn from the Pentagon, ACDA, the State Department and National Security Council to negotiate a partial test ban treaty they were ordered to report direct to the president, not to their own organizational heads.[57] Kennedy's personal involvement and direction led to the negotiations producing a Partial Test Ban Treaty within ten days.[58] A similar centralized control and direct commitment can be observed in the involvement of President Nixon and Henry Kissinger in the final negotiations leading to the SALT I treaties in 1972. A participant in the SALT I talks stressed the importance of the President's personal commitment in the attainment of a treaty: 'I would stress above all the need in negotiating with the Russians for firm leadership, direction and support for the negotiation from the president down.'[59]

Conclusion

Henry Kissinger noted with regard to the diplomacy of the early nineteenth century that it was paradoxical that 'Metternich had greater difficulty with the Austrian than with the Russian ministers, and that in every negotiation Castlereagh had to fight a more desperate battle with his Cabinet than with his foreign colleagues.'[60] In this respect, as in others, little has changed in the world of international politics. Domestic influences continue to play a leading role in determining whether or not arms control is possible and, if it is possible, how much can be contemplated. The domestic arena and the political realities of that arena have to be borne in mind at all times, and explain many of the arms control postures adopted by governments. Politics is about power, position and influence over outcomes, and arms control is just another form of politics. Domestic factors do not give the entire explanation as to why arms control seems to have delivered so little, however. It is necessary to look also at the other side of the bargaining coin: that is, at the way in which negotiations with the arms control adversary/partner are carried out.

6

Bargaining with the Adversary

There has been 'a growing skepticism that negotiation can modify significantly the US–Soviet military competition.

Lewis, *The Economics of SALT Revisited*[1]

Introduction

Arms control negotiations between the superpowers are now seen as representing business as usual. Western publics become uneasy if negotiations are stalled for any length of time or if an administration seems reluctant to enter into such negotiations. Where once arms control talks were a remarkable exception to the norm of international politics, now they are viewed as being an essential element of international diplomacy. So firmly rooted is this conceptualization, it has been argued that 'even if the failure of arms control and disarmament talks is obvious from the beginning, governments deem it appropriate to engage in them.'[2]

This resilient public support for the idea of arms control negotiations is all the more remarkable given the paucity of the results of nearly 30 years of effort. In that period no mutually acceptable definition of strategic security has emerged, no significant reductions in weaponry have occurred and both sides continue to feel threatened by what they view as the destabilizing weapons programmes of the adversary. The question of why, in these circumstances, governments remain so enamoured of arms control negotiations is looked at in chapter 8; the purpose of this chapter is to analyse why the *process*, which the general public supports so strongly, has so signally failed to achieve the goals the public associates with the effort: that is, greater stability, reduced tension and significant decreases in weaponry, particularly in nuclear warhead totals.

Clearly some governments have been rather more enthusiastic about the pursuit of arms control than others. Yet overall the results have not differed a great deal, and this raises the suspicion that the very nature of arms control bargaining between adversaries mitigates against the attainment of arms control ends. The manner in which the superpowers have chosen to conduct their arms control dialogue may well be entirely unsuited to the task, so that the actual process of negotiation has on occasion made the situation worse rather than better.

The Microscope Effect

During the 1970s the superpowers explored the possibility of a military–political accommodation in a variety of fields. A large number of negotiations took place including those on conventional forces in Europe, biological weapons, chemical weapons, anti-satellite weapons, arms transfers, naval manoeuvres, ballistic missile defences, strategic nuclear weapons, intermediate-range nuclear weapons, seabed-emplaced nuclear weapons, and so on. While most of these negotiations had intrinsic value and were designed to produce a more stable strategic environment, they had the unlooked-for side-effect of concentrating attention upon the details of each side's military potential. Thus even in an activity which sought a cooperative approach to security, the effect was to accentuate still further the salience of the military aspect of the superpower relationship. This resulted to a large extent in the field of interest being 'narrowed down to the most conflict loaded issues'.[3]

This effect was increased by the fact that the superpowers chose parity as the basic objective in their negotiations. Parity is a perfectly logical and reasonable goal to strive for and it enables the participants to suggest a coherent structure with their proposals and to justify any resulting treaty or agreement to their own population. Parity can, however, become a fetish and the attempt to produce parity at all levels carries dangers within it. As Michael Krepon has noted, 'the quest for parity can, however, become an exercise in futility if it means matching detailed weapon system characteristics rather than aggregate force levels.'[4]

The pursuit of 'optical parity', that is the existence of equal weaponry totals in all areas, is both futile in itself and unnecessary in practice. It is a futile objective because the superpowers can never have armed forces that are the exact mirror-image of each other. For a variety of geographical, political, strategic and economic reasons naval power is far more important to the US than the Soviet Union, whereas the Soviet Union needs huge land forces while the US does not. Even in the area of strategic nuclear weaponry, factors such as geography, history, technological development rates, strategic theory, bureaucratic politics and administrative inertia mean that the nuclear deterrents of each side have developed in different ways, the Soviet Union preferring to place most of its warheads on land-based ICBMS while maintaining a minimal manned bomber force, and the US limiting its ICBM deployments and maintaining a large bomber force. Each side has good reasons of its own for developing its preferred 'mix' of weapons and neither is prepared to distort its force posture by aping that of the other side purely in order to achieve optical parity in all systems.

Any negotiating strategy which has as its goal the aim of getting the other side to adopt one's own force posture is therefore doomed to failure. This, however, is precisely the strategy which the US has been pursuing for the past 30 years. It has not quite argued that 'what's good for the US is good for the world', but the end result has been just about the same. US negotiators have consistently argued that the particular mix of weapon systems and development pattern adopted by their nation is inherently more stable than that preferred by the Soviet Union. If one accepts the arcane logic of deterrent theorists about the preferability of secure second-strike systems over first-strike systems then the US position is impossible to argue with. However, since the US was essentially arguing for bombers and submarines and against ICBMs, in practice it was saying that in order to attain strategic stability it must keep what it had, while the Soviet Union must scrap much of what it had, but the Soviets would be free to build lots of expensive new bombers and submarines, which they had never favoured.

Not surprisingly, therefore, the Soviet Union came to feel that the US criteria for dividing weapons into those which were stabilizing and those which were not were artificially contrived in order to limit the weapons preferred by the Soviet Union while allowing a more or less free rein to those favoured by the US.[5] While it was valid to attempt to educate Soviet leaders as to the implications of their force posture, it was counterproductive to formulate arms control proposals which attempted to force the Soviet Union to adopt preferred US strategies.

Parity at all levels was not even a necessary objective. What is required for successful mutual deterrence is a balance of capabilities in which neither side has the capacity to inflict a disarming first strike on the other. So long as neither side can do this, while both sides have ample retaliatory capability with which to destroy an aggressor, then a stable balance exists. Within this overall balance of capabilities it does not matter if there are differences in each side's strategic architecture; for example one side has more ICBMs, the other more SLBMs. As long as these differences do not give either side a first-strike capability then the fact that there is an overall balance, parity at the highest level, is all that matters. US Secretary of Defense Schlesinger noted in 1974 that numerical parity in strategic nuclear weapons was not a military necessity, though it might be desirable for domestic political reasons.[6]

The pursuit of parity has had a further unfortunate impact upon arms control negotiations. Since states do not like having to dismantle expensively acquired military hardware, parity is invariably arrived at by allowing the weaker of the adversaries in any particular category to catch up, rather than by having the stronger of the two cut back its weapon totals. Thus, for example, in the 1972 ABM treaty the Soviets were given the right to build a second ABM site and the US were allowed to build two to maintain parity, rather than the Soviets being encouraged to produce parity at zero by dismantling the only ABM site then in existence (near Moscow). Vice-President Mondale criticized the Vladivostok accords on offensive weapons for similar reasons, arguing that although, as Kissinger had claimed, Vladivostok put a cap on the arms race, 'the cap was fifteen feet over the head. The Vladivostok agreement was basically a matter of taking the force levels of the two sides, adding fifteen percent, and stapling them together.'[7]

The parity thus arrived at then has a tendency to be seen as the floor for subsequent bargaining, rather than the ceiling.[8] The pursuit of parity has thus tended to make for arms control agreements which do little more than legitimize the ongoing weapons programmes of the two sides. While this may be negotiable and may not harm strategic stability, it does little or nothing to convince the ordinary citizen that things are getting better.

Unfortunately public attitudes are themselves partly to blame for the parity obsession. As noted earlier, the general public is generally supportive of arms control but is often a stern critic of particular agreements. For democracies in particular it is important not to be seen to have been 'sold a pup'. Parity established via overall aggregate levels is fine in theory, but the political reality is that if, in certain sub-categories, the other side seems to have been allowed an advantage, then the government becomes politically vulnerable. This was clearly the case with the SALT I agreement where the Nixon administration produced a package which essentially balanced a Soviet advantage in launchers against a US advantage in warheads. The agreement was attacked in the Senate by Senator Jackson who focused on the fact that the Soviets retained their monopoly of large 'heavy' ICBMs. Although the Nixon administration pointed out that the US had no need for heavy ICBMs because their missiles were more accurate than the Soviet Union's, Jackson's simplistic arguments proved effective. The Senate insisted that in any future agreement there should be no significant disparity in sub-totals, thus vastly complicating the task of the US negotiators and reducing the chances of successful future agreements. The latter effect may indeed have been the object of the exercise as far as the drafters of the Jackson Amendment were concerned.

Bargaining Chips

In any demonology of arms control, the ubiquitous bargaining chip deserves a prominent position. A bargaining chip is a weapon or defence system which adversaries fear so much that they would be willing to make significant concessions in order to prevent it being adopted. The term can also be used to describe a system that one side feigns interest in believing that the other side will be sufficiently concerned to want to trade concessions in order to prevent its deployment.[9]

Those who favour the concept of bargaining chips argue that it is only the desire to constrain these weapon systems which brings the other side to the bargaining table in a mood to make concessions. Without the existence of Western systems capable of being bargained away, the Soviet Union would never agree to any limitations on its own forces. In support of this thesis proponents point to numerous US weapons programmes which appear to have been instrumental in encouraging the Soviets to negotiate. Thus, for example, the Soviet leadership showed no inclination to discuss a ban on BMD in the late 1960s. At the Glassboro Summit in 1967 Prime Minister Kosygin vehemently rejected a proposal for such a ban, saying that 'defense is moral, offense is immoral'.[10] Only after the Senate voted to approve an American ABM system in 1969 did the Soviet Union come to favour the idea of limiting ABMs. Similarly, the Soviets pressed ahead with unilateral programmes in ASAT weapons and INF during the 1970s and only began enthusing about negotiated limits when comparable US programmes were set in motion. Most dramatic of all, President Reagan's SDI led the Soviet Union to unfold a series of dramatic proposals, culminating in Mikhail Gorbachev's suggestion of a negotiated abolition of nuclear weapons over a 15-year period.[11] The proposal first made in January 1986 was reiterated in November 1986, with a ten-year timescale. President Reagan failed to cash in his bargaining chip, however, astonishing many SDI supporters who had never seen the programme as anything else and who felt that the US would never be offered a better deal. As one critic, former Secretary of State Cyrus Vance, declared, 'The President should have taken the deal because SDI was a bargaining chip, and that's the way it should have been played.'[12]

Those who doubt the value of bargaining chips argue that weapons programmes, far from encouraging the other side to negotiate, simply encourage them to seek matching weapon developments. This, they assert, is a prudent step to take because in practice bargaining chips are virtually never cashed in. Thus, for example, Secretary of State Henry Kissinger confessed that he had supported the strategic cruise missile programme because he saw the weapon as a valuable bargaining chip for the SALT negotiations, but he found that the Pentagon was not subsequently prepared to negotiate the weapons away in bargaining with the Soviet Union.[13] This view is corroborated by Gerard Smith, the chief US SALT I negotiator.[14] In a similar fashion the Trident submarine programme was initially defended as a bargaining chip in order to stifle congressional opposition.[15]

The only clear example of a bargaining chip successfully bringing concessions from the adversary and not subsequently being deployed was the Safeguard ABM system, which was cashed in to produce the 1972 ABM Treaty. It can be argued that the Soviet Union was losing confidence in its own *Galosh* ABM technology anyway by the early 1970s, and that Soviet deployment plans for ABM 'were already in a state of suspended animation'.[16] However, in the absence of the threatened US programme Soviet bureaucratic momentum would almost certainly have ensured the continued development of the programme.

The ABM treaty is very much the exception to the rule, however. Bargaining chips do not normally remain undeployed in this way. According to former ACDA director and chief SALT II negotiator, Paul Warnke, bargaining chips 'lead to agreements to arm rather than agreements on arms control'.[17] In the same hearings, however, Paul Nitze, later one of President Reagan's chief negotiators, defended bargaining chips by arguing that successful bargaining was impossible without them.[18]

Whether bargaining chips are useful or not depends to some extent on how you define them. A weapon system that is valued by its sponsors but which they are willing to bargain away in certain circumstances is a useful commodity, but a system which is being developed with no specific rationale other than the hope that the other side will fear it enough to make concessions is of dubious value. If the other side do not believe you have any use for the system they are unlikely to fear it themselves, and neither are they likely to be over-impressed by the retention of obsolescent systems for bargaining purposes. After the initiation of superpower negotiations on INF the Soviet Union halted its programme of withdrawing the ancient SS-4 and SS-5 missiles as the new SS-20s were deployed. It was clear to NATO that these old missiles were being retained beyond their useful life simply so that they could be traded away in an INF deal, thereby protecting a few SS-20s. However, since NATO could see this clearly, US negotiators were hardly likely to be sidetracked from their desire to curb the SS-20s merely by the offer of a few SS-4s. Similar thinking led NATO to begin withdrawing large numbers of obsolescent battlefield nuclear weapons from 1979. Since both sides were well aware of their age and limited value it was not thought worth hanging on to them as bargaining chips. As Robert Einhorn has put it, 'states will not give up their front-line systems in exchange for the other side's dinosaurs.'[19]

Neither, in practice, will states give up a weapon system once it has begun to show military promise, even if it had previously been promoted purely as a bargaining chip. The US development of MIRV gave them a clear technological lead over the Soviet Union for a few years, but no serious effort was made to use this to gain bargaining leverage and in time the MIRV acquired such a powerful array of defenders within the Pentagon that any possibility of limitations on this type of technology disappeared.

Bargaining chips enter into the broader question of what exactly provides bargaining leverage in negotiations and the strategy of 'negotiating from strength'. Simply piling up vast arrays of weaponry is not enough; the historical record of superpower arms control shows that the Soviet Union is more impressed by some types of technology than others, more concerned about US technological breakthroughs than about adding larger numbers of existing weapons types, and is quite prepared to do deals on occasion when the US has no bargaining advantages at all.[20]

In the early 1970s two major arms control agreements were signed on issues where the Soviet Union had little or no apparent need to make concessions. In the 1972 Biological Weapons Convention the Soviets agreed to the destruction of existing weapon stocks even though the US had unilaterally disarmed in this category in 1969. In 1974 the Soviets signed a Protocol to the ABM Treaty whereby they gave up their right to a second ABM site even though Congress had already refused funds for a second US site. Bargaining leverage is thus not always essential to produce an agreement.

Generally speaking, however, the Soviet Union usually prefers to see equal sacrifice for equal benefits in its dealings with the US. They have shown a tendency to fear the implications of actual or potential new technologies, and a willingness to constrain their existing programmes as the price for buying US restraint. This pattern is clearly visible in their reaction to US BMD programmes in the early 1970s and mid-1980s. Similar opportunities arose with MIRV and strategic cruise missiles, although in the latter cases the US was not tempted to exploit their bargaining potential. The Soviet Union does not appear to be particularly alarmed about overall numbers of strategic nuclear delivery vehicles and will therefore not give up much simply in order to prevent the US making marginal additions to its inventory. What has alarmed the Soviet leadership are US efforts which threatened to open up new avenues of competition in which the US was likely to maintain an advantage.

Their opponent's technological breakthroughs are a nightmare for the Soviet leadership because they require rapid redistribution of budgetary resources and technological effort, a response the Soviet system is ill-equipped to provide, as well as threatening unmanageable economic difficulties. Rather than get into an unforeseen and open-ended competition of this sort, the Soviet Union will adopt one of two strategies, sometimes pursuing both sequentially. The first option is to attempt to exploit Western political divisions in such a way that the programme is blocked. Such an effort was mobilized successfully against the Enhanced Radiation/Reduced Blast Weapon (the so-called 'neutron-bomb') in the late 1970s, but was less successful against the NATO INF programme between 1979 and 1983 or against President Reagan's SDI. Only if this strategy fails will the Soviet Union move to its second option, an arm control agreement involving mutual concessions.

There are problems for the Soviet Union in relying upon Western legislatures to restrain NATO governments, however. European governments are more vulnerable in this respect than US administrations but even they are difficult to exert pressure upon. The apparently fragile coalition governments in Italy, Holland and Belgium went ahead and approved the commitment to deploy cruise missiles on their respective territories despite Soviet threats and vocal anti-nuclear protests. In the US any Soviet praise for one of their politicians is an electoral kiss-of-death, so the Soviet leadership has to rely upon congressional wisdom to manifest itself spontaneously. This may happen but it cannot be relied upon, neither can its effectiveness be predicted or its continuity be assumed. Thus while it is true that the Soviet Union is less likely to offer concessions at the bargaining table if they feel that Congress will block a feared programme anyway, it is also true that they cannot rely on Congress. Congress has a poor record as far as abolishing weapons programmes is concerned and while the Soviets may hope for restraint imposed by

Congress it is not something that they can rely on sufficiently to factor it into their calculations.

It is worth noting also that failure to restrain the US at this early stage in a bargaining sequence pushes Soviet leaders across a critical threshold. Although they may make considerable efforts to block or negotiate constraints on a technology prior to deployment, once such a total ban has failed they often attach little further importance to constraints. Once forced to run they find it difficult to slow down again. In a number of issue areas therefore – MIRV, ABM, strategic cruise missiles and ASATs – a window of opportunity has existed prior to flight-testing which is virtually impossible to close again once that crucial threshold has been crossed.

Bargaining Tactics

The way in which arms control negotiations are conducted, that is to say the strategy and tactics employed by each side, can have a profound influence upon eventual outcomes. One factor which clearly has affected the success rate of such negotiations is the fact that there has been no clear consensus on what the real purpose of arms control talks is. The general attitude towards negotiations has varied widely, with some seeing communication between adversaries as being so important that talks are deemed valuable and the search for agreement vital almost irrespective of the final terms of any treaty. Others have seen negotiations as being a danger, an anaesthetic whose only real impact is to lull vigilance against the continuing machinations of the adversary. In between these two extremes have been those who credit arms control negotiations with varying degrees of limited utility.

Even within this central range of opinion there are wide varieties of outlook. While most see negotiations leading to agreement as a useful technique for fine-tuning the stability of the strategic balance, others see negotiations as simply another battleground, another weapon in the cold war.[21] These differing outlooks affect the tactics employed at negotiations and in turn have had a major impact on outcomes. For example, the US has on several occasions made generous offers to the Soviet Union on the assumption that they would be rejected and been forced into humiliating retreats from these positions when the Soviet

Union has looked on them positively. In the early stages of the SALT I talks a US suggestion for a complete ban on ABMS was abandoned after an initial Soviet display of interest in the idea.[22] Similarly, another proposal to abolish all nuclear weapons made at the 1986 Reykjavik summit was rapidly downgraded to one to ban ballistic nuclear missiles only, because the original offer was too similar to the concurrent Soviet proposal and therefore ran the risk of being accepted, an outcome which would have rocked NATO to its foundations.

Despite the fact that superpower arms control negotiations have been a feature of the adversarial partnership for a quarter of a century, there is still a tendency to adopt bargaining tactics suitable only for one-off situations. This attitude ignores the reality that tactics designed to obtain short-term gains are unlikely to affect the strategic relationship in a significant way: that is, the cost of alienating the other side will not be justified by a major and lasting strategic gain. In addition such tactics have a knock-on effect, leaving residual animosities which affect future relations and future bargaining sequences.

To adopt strategies that offer the greatest long-term gains is particularly difficult for democracies. Changes in administration can mean the arrival in government of individuals hostile to arms control as a whole, or to particular treaties or negotiations. Even when the incoming administration favours arms control it is likely to adopt new goals and tactics in order to emphasize the break with the previous administration. This will have the effect of interrupting stable bargaining sequences, as the arrival of the Carter administration did in 1977. Democracies are also hampered by a lack of patience which makes them want to achieve a great deal quickly, preferably in a single package, rather than accept a gradual evolution in the desired direction. Thus critics of the SALT II treaty argued that it was only a marginal improvement on SALT I, rather than accepting it as a useful gain and a further step in the desired direction which could be pursued in SALT III, SALT IV and so on. Frequent small steps are better than infrequent large ones because they are easier to negotiate and because they carry smaller political risks if problems arise. Moreover by occurring more frequently they make the nature of the process under way more visibile and the pay-offs more regular, so that gains made in one area – for example, concessions on verification

– can have a more rapid impact upon subsequent negotiations. The implication of this, as Christopher Makins has noted, is that it may well be desirable to break up issues into small negotiating packages even when they are logically linked to larger issues.[23]

In practice, when they have taken the long-term view, the super-powers to date have erred on the side of caution. They have tended to avoid making too many conciliatory moves in order not to acquire a reputation for weakness at the bargaining table. President Reagan deliberately chose Edward Rowney and Paul Nitze to head his arms control negotiating teams, two individuals who had strongly criticized previous US negotiators for being overeager to reach agreement.[24] This attitude is influenced by the assumption that the US desire for an agreement will be exploited by the Soviet negotiators. Thus, it is argued, if the US gives the impression that it badly needs an agreement with the Soviet Union, the Soviets are unlikely to feel that they will have to make concessions if agreement is to be reached. If, on the other hand, the US gives the impression that it would like an agree-ment, but would be prepared to do without one, then Soviet con-cessions become a precondition to any treaty.[25] By the same line of reasoning 'strong' US presidents are more likely to induce Soviet concessions than weak ones because they can credibly threaten a compensating arms build-up if a satisfactory arms control agreement is not forthcoming, and because public and political opinion will trust such an agreement if a hawkish president has signed it.[26] President Nixon exploited this situation to conclude an array of agreements with the Soviet Union in the early 1970s.

There has tended to be a marked discrepancy in preferred nego-tiating tactics between presidents and their bureaucracies. The career diplomats in the State Department have felt that the best way forward was by small, frequent steps. Their political superiors have invariably felt that dramatic sweeping gestures were preferable. Thus, for example, in 1977 while President Carter and National Security Adviser Brzezinski favoured abandoning the SALT II framework produced by Kissinger even though it was 90 per cent complete and instead opted for a radical new initiative, Secretary of State Vance favoured his department's position, which was to go for an early agreement along the lines already mapped out by Kissinger.[27] Unfotunately Vance's view did not prevail. Had it done so a SALT II agreement much along the lines of the 1979 treaty, but with bipartisan support, would have been in place in 1977. On the evidence of the 1982 Soviet START proposal, Carter could probably even have negotiated a SALT III agreement, simply implementing further across-the-board cuts of 10 per cent, before he left office in 1981. Had this happened the track-record of the SALT process, and of multi-lateral disarmament, would have looked a lot better than in practice it did when President Reagan inherited the stalled SALT II agreement in 1981.

One reason for the failure of President Carter's 1977 proposals was that it ignored the concessions made by the Soviet Union which enabled the Kissinger–Ford SALT II treaty to be put together. The Soviets felt that Carter had shown scant regard for the political effort Brezhnev made in getting the agreement's outlines accepted within the Kremlin bureaucracy. The difficulties in getting a domestic bureaucracy to accept a negotiated arms control package were discussed in the previous chapter and, bearing these in mind, the dismay occasioned to the bargaining partner when the whole elaborate deal is subsequently abandoned in favour of a fresh start can be imagined.

The complexity of formal negotiating sequences and their vulnerability to the shifting sands of international politics have led some observers to question the value of the formal negotiation itself, arguing that there is considerable evidence in favour of the belief that formal negotiations are actually a hindrance to the achievement of mutual limitations.[28] One sceptic has drawn attention to the fact that the pursuit of disarmament by formal international negotiations was a technique bequeathed by the 'mentally unbalanced' Tsar Nicholas II of Russia.[29] The historical record of such negotiations in fact goes a great deal further back than this; thousands of years in the case of the Chinese warring states.[30] This caveat aside there is no denying the validity of the same critic's argument that, given the dismal record of results obtained by the formal diplomatic approach, there is 'a strong *prima facie* case for its criticial re-examination'.[31]

It is worth reminding ourselves, therefore, that although we have grown used to seeing arms control pursued in this way, the early proponents of arms control specifically noted that more informal methods existed, and in many circumstances felt these would be more appropriate. Thomas Schelling and Morton Halperin in the seminal work, *Strategy and Arms Control*, published in 1961, argued that to be truly effective the varieties of control mechanisms had to be as numerous as the problems they were required to control and that a flexible concept of arms control was necessary which accepted that 'the degree of formality may range from a formal treaty with detailed specifications at one end of the scale, through executive agreements, explicit but informal understandings, tacit understandings, to self-restraint that is consciously contingent on each other's behaviour.'[32] Similarly, Fred Iklé argued in 1964 that formal negotiations could do more harm than good if they introduced 'political issues or questions of prestige and legal precedents' and that therefore agreements arrived at without formal negotiations should be sought when they were appropriate.[33]

While it is true that informal agreements are valuable, the emphasis (as Schelling and Halperin noted) should be on variety of techniques. Although it can be argued that 'informal, off the record, secret negotiations, in which decisions are made centrally and many bureaucratic actors are excluded, increase the prospects for a success-ful outcome',[34] in fact such informal techniques have their own pitfalls and drawbacks. The positive side is that flexibility is increased, decision-making time reduced and internal conflict is kept to a minimum. Thus, for example, the Kissinger–Dobrynin informal 'back-channel' led to the 1971 breakthrough in the SALT I nego-tiations.

However, the reverse side of the coin is that by failing to build a consensus around the positions adopted the administration makes itself vulnerable to domestic criticism which may cause future diffi-culties. Although such techniques enabled the SALT I negotiations to be brought to a comparatively rapid conclusion, they have been described as a model of how *not* to conduct negotiations, 'against a political deadline, by an ill-prepared political negotiation team (and without the best technical negotiating advice and assistance) seeking unattainable objectives and then settling for murky and ambiguous cosmetic formulations to cover over the situation'.[35]

The informal, or at least less rigidly formalized, approach would clearly work better if the subject matter under discussion was of the discrete, small-package variety alluded to earlier. The problems associated with the rush-to-print of the SALT I treaty were in large part due to the complexity and wide scope of the issues. A smaller, more manageable, issue area would involve less complexity and could therefore be finalized without the risks attendant upon a wide-ranging agreement.

Soviet Attitudes

The Soviet attitude towards arms control negotiations differs in certain significant ways from that of the US. The US defence community pays lip service to the idea that arms control and weapons acquisition can be complementary, each being pursued in any particular instance depending on whether it offers the most cost-effective route to enhanced security. In practice, however, hawks tend to feel that acquiring additional weapons is always a better bet than signing arms control treaties with the Soviet Union, while doves tend to feel suspicious of most (but not all) new weapons programmes and to feel that arms control is the preferable option most of the time. Only a minority argue that not only can the two approaches complement one another but also that both should be integrated within a broader vision of what the goals of US foreign policy should be at any particular time.

The Soviet Union in contrast does have an overarching vision of its foreign policy goals and can therefore more easily integrate all its potential foreign policy instruments. For this reason the Soviets view arms control as but one of a number of implements which are seen as mutually reinforcing. Significantly also the Soviet concept of 'the correlation of forces' is a much broader notion than the Western 'balance of power'. Whereas the latter is essentially a military balance, the correlation of forces embraces economic, social, political and ideological trends as well as the purely military. Soviet arms control goals reflect this so that they can seek objectives at negotiations which are not strictly military, and can trade military concessions themselves in the exception of non-military gains from the adversary. Thus arms control gains that 'elevate the USSR's international standing, weaken NATO's coherence, inhibit improvement in Sino–US relations, or undermine US public support for defence efforts may be seen by Soviet leaders as just as valuable as agreements that bring benefits in the more tangible military indicators of national strength'.[36]

A corollary of this Soviet attitude is that the Soviet Union does not always lay the emphasis on marginal military advantages that the

West might expect. The SALT I Interim Agreement gave the Soviet Union a numerical advantage over the US in terms of the number of ICBMs and SLBMs each side was allowed to possess. Critics argued that the perception of US inferiority would be played upon by the Soviets and thereby have a significant political impact. In fact, however, the Soviets made no effort to exploit the numerical advantage for propaganda purposes.[37] The only people who did try to undermine US morale in this way were the conservative critics of SALT I who consistently played up the significance of the Soviet launcher advantage, while ignoring the US warhead numbers superiority.

The Soviet Union is no less serious in arms control than is the US, and like its adversary tends to assess potential arms control issues in cost-benefit terms. The Soviets enter negotiations and conclude agreements if doing so would leave them better off than not doing so. However, the broader array of possible non-military gains alluded to earlier means that the cost-benefit equation will differ from the parallel US exercise. The Soviet government often takes a long time to decide whether or not to enter specific sets of negotiations, but once having committed themselves they negotiate in a serious manner. The initial hesitation invariably results from doubts about whether the US is itself serious.

Like the US the Soviet Union enters negotiations with the object of maximizing the constraints on the adversary while minimizing the constraints on itself. In practice the bargaining pattern of successive waves of concessions by both sides leading to agreements means that a final treaty is usually a bargain in which both sides have made roughly comparable concessions. One reason why the record of arms control achievement has been so thin to date is that neither side is primarily concerned with constraining the weapons held by the other side. Both sides feel that their own planned deployments, if implemented, will increase their own security without significantly compromising that of the other side. Even SDI, a programme specifically designed to neutralize the effectiveness of the Soviet deterrent and thereby leave the Soviet Union vulnerable to an US nuclear attack, has been defended in these terms. It is not possible, however, to negotiate constraints on the other side while leaving one's own forces unconstrained. With the exception of the limited reductions involved in SALT II and INF the superpowers have chosen to leave

their own forces unconstrained and let the other side do likewise.[38]
The arms control agreements have therefore invariably set ceilings
which were higher than the totals possessed by each side at the time of
the agreement and would allow each side to carry out the force
improvements then under way.

The Soviet Union seems to have attached more importance to the
symbolism involved in attaining parity with the US than to the need
to constrain US strategic nuclear weaponry. It has, like the US,
sought parity at levels high enough to enable weapons programmes to
run their course. It is worth pointing out, however, that in the SALT
II treaty the US was allowed to increase its weapons totals slightly
while the treaty would have obliged the Soviet Union to dismantle
10 per cent of its nuclear inventory to come down to the agreed
second-phase level of 2,250 launchers. It is curious that the Senate
and President Reagan chose not to ratify a treaty which would have
had no effect on the US but would have reduced the scale of the Soviet
threat by 10 per cent. The absence of radical alterations in defence
postures occasioned by the kind of arms control that has been acceptable to the superpowers to date has led one critic to describe the
SALT II treaty as merely 'a photograph of the situation which has
arisen from the programmes of the two superpowers'.[39]

The Soviet Union also differs from the US in that it attaches more
importance to what might be called the atmospherics of arms control
negotiations and agreements. The Soviets derive satisfaction from the
mere fact that the US is forced to negotiate with them as the other
superpower. The US in contrast tends to focus on the narrow
technical aspects of the nuclear balance. Because of this agreements
can be sought where the impact upon weapon systems is small,
leaving the US arms control community dissatisfied, while the
general political overtones of the agreements conclusion may satisfy
the less concrete aims of the Soviet leadership. Certainly in the early
rounds of the SALT I talks the two sides found they were pursuing
quite different objectives, with the Soviets focusing on the political
meaning of any superpower accord relating to weaponry while the US
sought highly detailed militarily significant arms control.[40] One of the
benefits of the series of negotiations during the 1970s was that the two
sides gradually came to acquire a better understanding of the
differences in each other's approach. They also created a series of
breakthroughs on such issues as verification, an agreed terminology,

data exchanges and so on which established a framework for future negotiations.

Non-Agreement Objectives

A state which initiates negotiations with another may do so for a variety of reasons. There may be a desire to conclude an agreement, either full or limited, on some particular issues that divide them. However, a state may seek to give the impression that this is its objective when in fact there are other reasons. These may include the use of the talks as a propaganda platform, the desire to explore the adversary's attitudes and possibly obtain useful intelligence gains, the desire to divert public attention from domestic difficulties or international setbacks in other areas, a wish to deceive the adversary as to the depths of one's animosity or a wish to delay certain political developments by making progress on them a hostage to the fortune of progress in the negotiations.

Negotiations may also be of a mixed character, where the parties are genuinely seeking progress on a contentious issue if this is possible, but are at the same time exploiting the existence of the negotiations for some of the purposes mentioned above. A common feature of negotiations is for each side to suggest that the other is not genuinely interested in the central issue but simply pursuing peripheral objectives, particularly propaganda aims.

Propaganda gains are a primary motivation for states to participate in arms control negotiations. The negotiations for a comprehensive nuclear test ban conducted during the late 1950s certainly were more concerned with the desire to score propaganda points rather than any serious desire to conclude an agreement. Many proposals were submitted because they would seem superficially attractive to public opinion even though it was known in advance that they were totally unacceptable to the other side and therefore could not possibly form the basis for an agreement.[41] Similarly, one study of the UN Ten Nations Disarmament Committee described it as 'a classic example of the skilful use of propaganda as an alternative to serious bargaining'.[42]

Arms control negotiations have become a virtual sub-species of diplomacy. Because such negotiations are now an expected part of the

normal business of international politics the major powers have insti-
tutionalized their arms control negotiating within their foreign policy
bureaucracies. There are now permanent sections, departments and
agencies whose task is to keep abreast of technological developments,
political changes and doctrinal alterations and be able to provide their
governments at any time with the wherewithal to participate in actual
or potential negotiations.

Arms control negotiations have been a basic foreign policy instrument for many states, and particularly for the superpowers. They are
no longer simply a mechanism designed to enable states to grapple
with the implications of advances in military technology on either side
of the Iron Curtain; rather they have become avenues in which
adversary states attempt to gain traditional foreign policy goals while
focusing their manoeuvring in a single arena.

Such negotiations have therefore become increasingly burdened by
having to carry too many responsibilities simultaneously. A set of
negotiations like SALT II is expected not only to resolve the specific
strategic problems that are the crux of the talks, but in addition is
expected to be a propaganda platform, a vehicle for alliance mobiliz-
ation and leadership, a weathervane for the position of *détente* in the
superpower relationship, a means of demonstrating a commitment to
arms control to non-aligned states, a means of reassuring domestic
publics that attempts are being made to limit the economic burdens of
the arms race and reduce the dangers of war, while at the same time
demonstrating firmness and resolve and a willingness to compete to
the adversary. It is hardly surprising that arms control has staggered
under such a burden. Because arms control is the last chain the public
wishes to see broken when superpower relations sour it may at times
be virtually the only remaining continuous channel of dialogue open,
as the talks on Mutual and Balanced Force Reductions in Europe
were in the early 1980s.

Conclusions

Arms control negotiations between potential adversaries are ponderous
and complex. They are complicated both by the difficulties of
generating and maintaining domestic consensus behind negotiating
positions and by the problems inherent in trying to produce mutual

reassurance between states which profoundly mistrust one another. It is hardly surprising that the arms control agreements concluded to date have been modest in impact; they would never have emerged from the tangle of conflicting needs and objectives of the parties involved if there were any danger that they might have a radical impact.

It is historically highly unusual for states as hostile to one another as the superpowers to attempt to limit their own capacities for confronting the adversary. It is also paradoxical for states to attempt to negotiate agreements on relative strengths when, short of actually fighting a nuclear war, it is impossible to be absolutely certain what their relative strengths actually are.[43] With these difficulties in mind even President Carter's chief SALT negotiator, Paul Warnke (a committed arms control supporter), had to admit that arms control as far as international politics is concerned is essentially 'an unnatural act'.[44] The fact that the consequences of a nuclear war would make the latter a perversion of the first order, however, means that arms control will continue to be pursued. Nevertheless, even when an agreement has successfully run the gauntlet of the domestic and international bargaining processes, a final obstacle remains to be surmounted; this is the question of whether or not arms control agreements can be adequately verified by mutually distrustful states.

7

The Verification of Agreements

Verification is becoming a shield for those not interested in arms control to hide behind.

Graybeal, quoted in The Verification Challenge[1]

Introduction

Since the early 1960s the leaders of the NATO and WTO governments have felt obliged to pursue the goal of negotiated arms limitations with their ideological adversary. Since the early arms control initiatives emerged after a long period of cold war which had wreaked enormous damage on the images each side held of the other, the unfolding East–West relationship was marked by a profound absence of trust. It was to that extent inevitable therefore that the issue of 'verifiability' loomed large in the subsequent negotiations. During the Senate Hearings on the SALT II treaty, ACDA Director George M. Seignious testified that in the six years it had taken to negotiate the treaty verification issues had 'received more attention and more effort than any other single aspect of SALT policy'.[2]

All this effort was an attempt to produce treaties in which each side would be able to monitor the activities of the other side constantly in order to ensure that they were continuing to abide by the terms of the treaty. Without this provision regarding verification it would have been essentially impossible for the signatories to conclude such crucial agreements with partners they did not entirely trust.

It has not always been an automatic assumption that arms control treaties require careful verification; indeed, the US was itself one of the last of the Great Powers to adopt this point of view. The US Navy Secretary rejected the idea of on site inspection (OSI) to verify the 1922 Washington Naval Treaty, saying that verification was 'undesirable and may be provocative of friction'.[3] Similarly, in 1927 the administration of President Coolidge believed that any treaty which relied upon verification because of an underlying distrust would not only fail to attain its goals but would itself contribute new suspicions and bad feeling.[4] By 1969, however, President Nixon felt obliged to instruct his SALT I negotiating team that 'any agreed limitations must therefore meet the test of verifiability.'[5]

Some categories of military activity by their very nature are more difficult to monitor than others. It is comparatively easy to monitor an atmospheric nuclear test ban, but extremely difficult to monitor a ban on the production of chemical munitions. Clearly, therefore, the negotiations about verification requirements will be more crucial and more difficult for some treaties than for others. These very real problems are bound to slow down the pace of the negotiations no matter how earnest each side is about reaching an agreement.

Critics of the glacial pace of the arms control negotiations during the 1970s have argued, however, that while verification difficulties have frequently been cited as the major impediment to progress, this has not in fact been the case. Rather, they argue, governments – and most notably the government of President Reagan – used the verification issue as an excuse to delay entering into any arms control agreements at all.[6] This was achieved by insisting that arms control is desirable only when it can be effectively verified and then establishing criteria for effective verification which simply cannot be met. Certainly the 1980s witnessed the verification issue raised from being an important element in arms control to being perhaps the most central issue in terms of the public debate. Many commentators on this process have felt that the issue has begun to be taken out of perspective. Freeman Dyson, for example, has criticized those 'American technical experts and politicians who have made the details of verification systems more important than the substance of the agreements that were to be verified'.[7] Such an approach was notable, for instance, in the US proposals to the UN chemical weapons talks at Geneva, where the US ambassador argued that a verification and compliance framework should be agreed on before productive negotiations on an actual chemical arms control treaty could begin.[8] The Soviet Union by contrast has tended to argued that to accord verification such a determining role is to put the cart before the horse: that 'disarmament without control is impossible, but control without disarmament is senseless.'[9]

Clearly then the whole issue of verification is a major area of controversy within the debate about the value of arms control. At the same time, however, it is an issue which is by no means well understood and to illuminate the reasons why verification has become such a stumbling block it is necessary to explain what exactly verification is, and what it can and cannot be expected to achieve in the context of arms control agreements.

The Meaning of 'Verification'

Arms control verification is the process by which states utilize their intelligence gathering and interpretation capabilities for the purpose of satisfying themselves that their treaty partners are abiding by the terms of the agreements they have signed. The actual process of verification involves two distinct phases. The first of these is monitoring, the collection of information pertinent to the treaty partners' behaviour regarding the agreement in question. The second phase is evaluation, the point at which the data is analysed and interpreted in order to determine whether the treaty is in fact being complied with.

The existence of these two phases is crucial to the debate about verification. When argument about verification occurs it invariably relates to the *monitoring* process and the difficulties encountered in the physical collection of relevant data. Thus disputes revolve around the reliability of seismic monitoring equipment, the effectiveness of satellite photography, the number of telemetry monitoring stations required and so on.

However, the reality of the situation is that monitoring is not only merely one of the aspects of verification, it is not even the most important. There is no shortage of monitoring data. It is the second phase of analysis and assessment which is the real problem area, a fact which is certainly not appreciated by the wider public. Monitoring is a relatively straightforward technical exercise, an attempt to see what the other side is doing.[10] By contrast the real verification of agreements occurs in the second phase when subjective judgements have to be made about the meaning and implications of the data[11] not only in terms of what the evidence seems to indicate, but also of the meaning of the original treaty terms themselves.[12] The problems produced by this inherently subjective aspect of verification will be addressed later, but first it is worth looking at what verification is supposed to achieve and why governments feel it to be such a crucial component of arms control agreements.

Verification serves three interrelated purposes. These are:

1 to detect any variations from agreed arms limitations;
2 to act as a deterrent to violations and thereby ensure compliance;
3 to promote public confidence in arms control agreements.[13]

The objectives are clearly based upon certain assumptions. It is assumed that the treaty partner will attempt to cheat[14], that the risk of such cheating can be minimized by the careful scrutiny of the adversary's actions, and that one's own population will assume that the adversary will try to cheat, will need reassurance on this point and will therefore not support any arms control agreement which lacks mechanisms for ensuring that the other side abides by the terms of the agreement.

The promotion of public confidence is absolutely crucial. In this regard the Soviet Union has an advantage over the Western democracies in that when the Soviet government assures its people that Western compliance can be adequately verified, the absence of critics arguing publicly that this is not so means that government assurances suffice to allay any concerns the Soviet people might have. In the West, however, where verification is a highly-charged and heavily politicized issue for debate, public reassurance is much more difficult to achieve. Doubts about an agreement's verifiability can undermine public support for an agreement, whether those doubts are justified or not; because of this, opponents of the agreement on other grounds have a vested interest in encouraging such doubts. From the political point of view, moreover, the scale of any apparent breaches of the agreement do not matter, since any breaches once detected will feed doubts concerning the trustworthiness of the treaty partner.[15] A number of small breaches may be interpreted as part of a pattern with a wider military or political significance.[16]

The absence of trust in the security aspects of international relations means that arms control agreements have to be designed in such a way that the need for trust is minimized. Even supporters of arms control, such as former CIA Director William Colby, have felt obliged to declare that 'the first and most obvious fundamental is, of course, that we should not "trust" the Russians.'[17] Verification therefore acts as a substitute for trust.[18]

It is sometimes argued that verification, by proving compliance, fosters future trust and confidence in the existing arms control regime, producing a balance of power based on 'Mutual Assured Detection', so to speak. There is very little evidence for such developments in practice, however. On the contrary, the arguments of President Coolidge noted earlier seem to have been sustained: verification efforts derived from mistrust cannot overcome that mistrust and may in practice simply contribute to it.

Verification is an inherently subjective exercise and in practice government ministers and officials bring long established predispositions to bear on compliance issues. Thus, for example, between 1972 and 1980 the US was led by two Republican and one Democratic party presidents. All three, Nixon, Ford and Carter, mistrusted the Soviet Union to some extent, but assumed that the Soviets were negotiating seriously and would abide by their treaty commitments. Allegations of Soviet non-compliance with aspects of various treaties arose occasionally, were the subject of investigation or further negotiation and were resolved to the satisfaction of the US government. Under President Reagan, however, a different set of assumptions prevailed, which assumed that the Soviet Union was continuously cheating and that where no evidence for this could be found this simply meant that the Soviets had successfully camouflaged their duplicity. In the light of this attitude many complaints about Soviet behaviour which had been resolved prior to 1981 were resuscitated and new, unfavourable verdicts returned. Trust is a mental attitude. A basically trusting or non-trusting attitude will have taken form in a politician's character long before he or she reaches the highest positions of government. President Reagan's basic attitudes had been forming for nearly three-quarters of a century before he became president and were thus highly resistant to change, no matter how convincing the case for it.

Not only does the perceived need for verification indicate a continuing absence of trust, it is also predicated upon an unwillingness to assume that the treaty partner's motives for signing an agreement will be broadly similar to one's own. Essentially states pursue arms control as a cost-effective route to security. They do so when they feel that certain military activities by the other side are so alarming that a deal to constrain them is judged essential even though the price is that a certain amount of reciprocal self-restraint must be exercised as well. In addition the arms control route is pursued only when the 'arms race' alternative strategy is deemed unlikely to succeed for whatever reason. Indeed, a deal is possible only when both sides have reached this position more or less simultaneously, so that each has something to offer in return for the desired restraint by the other side.

Although in pursuing their bargaining strategies at the negotiations both sides tend to accept this as being the logic of the situation, in pursuing their verification demands they frequently lose sight of it. If both sides are negotiating because they fear something the other side has, then each has a powerful incentive to abide by the deal struck in order to maintain the constraints on the other side which would otherwise not exist. The logic of the verification demands, however, is that only the likelihood of detection prevents the other side from cheating because they have entered the bargain purely in order to reap the benefits that successful chicanery would bring.

The importance of these differing attitudes is that they demand quite different levels of verification accuracy. If a state is complying because it needs the treaty in place to restrain the other side, it is unlikely to cheat because if it was caught the treaty would collapse and the vital restraints be lost. In this case a much less than perfect verification apparatus should be necessary; one that simply ensures that detection is likely will suffice.

If a state has probably signed a treaty with an intention to cheat, however, then clearly a much higher standard of verification is necessary, one which raises the likelihood of detection close to certainty. The question then arises, is such certainly possible or even necessary?

The Subjective Element in Verification: How Much Certainty is Needed?

The verification of compliance with arms control agreements is a subjective activity. The technical exercise of monitoring produces large amounts of evidence – satellite and aircraft photos, radar images, seismic readings, signal telemetry recordings and so on – but the facts do not 'speak for themselves'. Having accumulated the data it is then necessary to analyse it, to sift through it to see whether it reveals a record of compliance, or whether there is evidence of attempts to deviate from the requirements of the treaty.

This is far harder than it sounds. Monitoring does not produce clear evidence of cheating; what it tends to give is a mass of evidence, most of which indicates compliance. Invariably, however, it will generate some evidence that is ambiguous or which might indicate that the treaty is not being adhered to. At this point additional information will be sought in order to clarify the apparent anomalies and some will be satisfactorily resolved. But there is still likely to remain a residue of evidence sufficient to warrant some suspicion.

This is always likely to be the case because treaties themselves invariably contain ambiguities. This may be due to careless drafting, to technical advances which were not anticipated at the time of the treaty, or to the states involved having deliberately chosen to leave certain clauses rather vague in order to maximize their future room for manoeuvre within the treaty's constraints. When states subsequently engage in activities impinging on the grey areas of the treaty there is clearly scope for disagreement about what exactly was or was not forbidden by the treaty. There will also be a certain amount of ambiguity caused simply by the very detailed discrimination capabilities that certain monitoring tasks require.

From time to time there will also be examples of activities which are technically treaty breaches but which are accepted by the other side because the breaches are clearly unintentional and unavoidable, or are temporary breaches caused by special conditions with no intent to gain a military advantage by deliberately circumventing the treaty. For example, in 1975 the Soviet Union complained that the US had constructed large prefabricated shelters covering some of its Minuteman II silos, a breach of Article 5 of the SALT I Interim Agreement which forbids deliberate concealment measures that impede verification by NTM. However, the Soviet Union accepted the US explanation that these were coverings designed to shelter workmen from the winter weather while work on the silos proceeded. In 1977 the US reduced the shelters in size by half in order to ease the Soviets' monitoring problem.

The real verification problems, however, arise when monitoring produces what appears to be evidence of non-compliance which is not a temporary or reasonable transgression; in other words, when the treaty partner appears to have been caught cheating. The problem here is that politically significant breaches of this sort are usually detected at the margins of monitoring capabilities so that the evidence is far from being clear-cut. Because of this reactions will be based upon existing conceptions of the treaty partner, producing a 'willingness to give the benefit of the doubt or to see suspicions confirmed'.[19] The nature of monitoring and interpretation is such that it cannot be an exercise in definitive proof.[20] On the contrary it is a thoroughly judgemental and political activity. Because most evidence is ambiguous, subjective judgements become crucial, and the more ambiguous the data, the greater the significance of subjective considerations becomes. In addition, because there must always remain some element of doubt attached to verification results, the crucial question is 'how much doubt can be tolerated, and at what point is ambiguity so unacceptable that it is unsafe to conclude an agreement?'

One of the reasons why verification became such a contentious issue after 1975 was that the US had never actually established clear guidelines as to what degree of verification uncertainty was acceptable for any particular treaty. Rather, successive adminstrations restricted themselves to a broad definition of what standard of verifiability they were aiming for in their arms control agreements as a whole. During the 1970s this standard was described as 'adequate verification' and was defined by President Nixon as a practical standard rather than an abstract ideal, based upon the ability to 'identify attempted evasion if it occurs on a large enough scale to pose a significant risk, and whether we can do so in time to mount a sufficient response'.[21]

The Nixon administration adopted a reasonable and realistic standard for verification, one which recognized that absolute certainty was impossible and that if monitoring requirements were made too demanding it would foreclose the possibility of any arms control agreements whatsoever. This standard of 'adequate' verification remained the objective under Presidents Ford and Carter. In the words of Admiral Inman, former Deputy Director of the CIA: 'If you insist on absolute certainty, if you insist on the capacity to detect every violation, you'll never have an arms control process. You have to take risks. The key is being confident that you will detect any serious cheating.'[22] Harold Brown, President Carter's Defense Secretary, expressed this confidence in terms of what he called 'the double bind': any cheating which could be successfully hidden would have to be so small as to be militarily insignificant, whereas the more significant the effort, the more likely it was to be detected by the other side.[23] It was on the basis of this standard that the administration was able to say of the SALT II agreement that 'despite the closed nature of Soviet society, we are confident that no significant violation of the treaty could take place without the United States detecting it.'[24]

Critics of the 'adequate' verification criteria argued that it was insufficiently stringent, and called for much more demanding standards amounting to a requirement for absolute certainty. Richard Perle, for example, declared that a treaty was only truly verifiable 'if *any* behaviour inconsistent with the treaty' could be detected by the other party.[25] When President Reagan took office in 1981 this standard, described as 'effective' verification, became the new criterion replacing 'adequate' verification. The administration also informed Congress that it intended to hold negotiations with the Soviet Union specifically limited to the question of establishing general principles and practices regarding the types of verification to be employed in any future arms control agreements.[26]

Surprisingly, however, this reformulation was not translated into concrete arms control initiatives. When the administration made public its proposals for the START and INF negotiations they contained no mention of verification provisions, a deficiency which provoked criticism. In subsequent years verification proposals were linked to the administration's arms control initiatives, but these intensified rather than reduced the criticism since they seemed to indicate that the administration was using stringent verification demands in order to avoid concluding arms control agreements, or at the very least was so lacking in enthusiasm for arms control that it cared little if its verification demands rendered progress almost impossible.

On some issues the Reagan administration announced that effective verification was impossible. Thus, for example, the negotiations on a CTB were ended because of verification difficulties, though the nature of these difficulties was not explained. Similarly, the administration initially refused to enter ASAT talks because an ASAT treaty could not be verified, although they did not say why this was so. When congressional pressure forced an explanation that an ASAT treaty could not be monitored unless all satellites were banned, Senator Larry Pressler pointed out that this bizarre suggestion was comparable 'to refusing to limit nuclear weapons until all airliners are taken out of service'.[27]

In other areas a treaty was proposed, but with verification requirements of impossible stringency. For example, the administration's proposals for a chemical weapons ban contained verification proposals so intrusive that no US government would ever have been able to implement them, much less a Soviet goverment; indeed, some of the proposals contained therein might actually have been illegal under the US constitution.[28]

Not surprisingly, proposals so patently incapable of implementation gave rise to the suspicion that an eventual agreement on arms control formed no part of the administration's objectives. Arms control negotiations may be pursued for reasons other than that of reaching an agreement, of course, and some of these tangential objectives – intelligence gathering, bridge-building and so on – may themselves be valuable goals. In general, however, it is assumed that states entering negotiations have some eventual agreement in mind and have at least an outline idea of what they are prepared to trade off and compromise on to achieve such an agreement. The Reagan administration gave no such impression. If it was not deliberately proposing verification terms designed to be rejected then it was at the very least undermining the agreement goal by breaking the fundamental guideline in such matters: that is, 'monitoring standards should not be so exacting as to foreclose agreement.'[29]

By the beginning of his second term there was some evidence that President Reagan's desire for an arms control agreement of some sort was on the increase and that he had recognized that the criteria laid down for 'effective' verification between 1981 and 1985 would in fact preclude any agreement. At a White House press conference on 9 January 1985 he declared that 'we also know that absolute verification is impossible.' It was noticeable that the definition of verification which appeared in the 1985 volume of Arms Control Impact Statements bore a striking resemblance to those of the 1970s administrations, defining verification as 'the process of determining, to the extent necessary to *adequately* safeguard national security, that the other side is complying with an agreement'.[30]

One reason for the change of emphasis may have been the belated realization that absolute certainty in verification was an unattainable goal. Indeed, taken to extremes such a goal was a logical absurdity. A leading architect of the initial demand for 'effective' verification was Amron Katz, a former ACDA official, who had argued that 'we have never found anything that the Soviets have successfully hidden.'[31] The appeal of this simplistic notion is that it is inherently unprovable. There is no evidence to support such a contention in the sense that the US has never subsequently discovered a major Soviet weapons advantage that it did not detect at the time, but to an adherent of the Katz approach this would prove the point. If Katz is correct one can only marvel at the restraint shown by the Soviet Union in not exploiting their hidden military supremacy in the past two decades.

The point about Katz's *reductio ad absurdum*, however, is that someone with that degree of suspicion is incapable of being reassured. The 'effective' verification goal pursued by such proponents is an impossible aim because you would never know when you had achieved it. Would the absence of evidence of cheating prove you had attained 'effective' verification or imply that the adversary's camouflage was still too good for your monitoring techniques? When looking at the effectiveness of monitoring technology, therefore, it is important to bear in mind that monitoring data can only establish reasonable certainty in either direction; it cannot establish absolute certainty because of the subjectivity inherent in the evaluation process. Verification is controversial because it is political and 'most controversies over questions of verification centre not on technical facts but on the evaluation of those facts in the larger context of policy.'[32] Even so, the capabilities of monitoring technology play a crucial role from the point of view of building domestic support for arms control agreements because of the public's perception of their capabilities.

The Effectiveness of 'Monitoring' Technology

A state's ability to monitor compliance with arms control agreements is as good as its general intelligence gathering capability, since the same technologies are used for both. Even if the superpowers never conducted arms control negotiations they would still monitor each other's military capabilities. The only difference would be that the data would be harder to obtain since the other side would then be free to disguise its activities to the maximum extent possible. It is only in the context of arms control negotiations that the NATO and WTO states have been prepared to discuss procedures for easier monitoring of each other's territories, and there is no doubt that arms control agreements ease the intelligence gathering task, irrespective of other benefits they may bring (a fact remarked upon by Secretary of State Cyrus Vance during the SALT II hearings).[33] In the modern world, where warning of attack relies upon remote technical devices such as satellites, anything which eases the task of these technologies is clearly to be welcomed.

This is an incidental benefit, however. The central question, of whether monitoring technology is adequate to enable arms control agreements to be entered into safely, is a focus for animated debate.[34] Clearly the question of how good the technology is depends to some extent on what exactly you expect it to do, and therefore identical monitoring capabilities may be seen as sufficient for someone demanding 'adequate' verification but be deemed unsatisfactory for someone looking for 'effective' verification. In addition there are various types of monitoring, some of which make greater demands upon the available technology than others. For analytical purposes, verification can be sub-divided in terms of the approach employed into the following categories:

1 traditional intelligence gathering (diplomatic techniques, media scrutiny, espionage);
2 national technical means;
3 on-site-inspection, (OSI).

The third category can itself be sub-divided[35] in terms of the degree of intrusiveness involved into:

1 remote OSI (seismic devices, prepositioned cameras and so on);
2 limited OSI (inspections limited to challenge);
3 interval OSI (regular periodic visitations);
4 residential OSI (permanent observation at certain points by observers);
5 unlimited zonal inspection (unlimited inspection rights in certain defined zones).

Thus only national technical means and remote OSI are completely reliant upon technology to provide their data. The actual types of technology which are employed in the monitoring of arms control agreements are as diverse as the agreements themselves. They include satellites equipped for visual photography, infra-red (heat) detection, nuclear radiation detection and communications interception, high-flying aircraft performing similar tasks, ground-based electronic intelligence listening posts, seismic monitoring stations, ground-based radars (including those like the 'Backscatter' Cobra Dane radars which can 'see' over the horizon), airborne radars and radars and electronic monitoring devices carried aboard ships. It is this very diversity of monitoring capabilities which sustains confidence, allowing for 'multiple and duplicative methods of detection'.[36]

This duplication is important because all the monitoring technologies have certain limitations and much of the technology is very expensive, so that there are limits to how many of any one type are likely to be functioning at any one time. For example, it is often assumed that the superpowers have 24-hour photographic reconnaissance of each other's territory through satellites. This is very far from being the case. Because they are extremely expensive very few photo-reconnaissance craft are in space at any one time, and those that are survey only part of their target state on each orbit. Thus even when the USSR, for example, has a photographic satellite above it only a small portion of the country will be under surveillance, and if the satellite does detect something of interest it may be several days before its orbit again brings it above the same spot for another look. Fortunately such absences have little operational significance. For SALT II monitoring, for instance, the USSR could hardly build, arm, and camouflage a new ICBM silo in between satellite passes.

Other operational problems may be inherent in the technology. Visual photography is of little use at night and cannot penetrate through clouds. However, at such times other techniques may be brought into play: for instance, infra-red or multispectral photography. 'Pictures' produced by radar imagery can also be used through clouds or at night.[37]

Gaps in the data obtained from technology may be filled by traditional intelligence gathering techniques. In 1979 a senior US official admitted that America had sources inside the Soviet missile design bureaux and had correctly predicted every single Soviet ICBM before

it was tested openly.[38] Soviet monitoring equipment is some five
years behind that of the US, but since the US is a far more open
society Soviet monitoring requirements are not so demanding.

Generally speaking the technology available for arms control verification is very good and is constantly being improved. The emergence
of new weapon systems such as multiple warheads and cruise missiles
has made some of the monitoring tasks more difficult and the tension
between advances in weapons technology and advances in monitoring technology will continue to be a feature of the arms control
environment. Problems caused by such 'grey-area' technology can be
overcome, but they demand a willingness by states to consider more
cooperative verification techniques, deliberately doing things in such
a way as to ease the other side's monitoring problems. The 'counting
rules' in SALT II were an example of such cooperative behaviour:
the two sides worked out ways to determine warhead numbers
present in each flight-tested missile.[39] Given the will to do so virtually
any verification monitoring problem can be overcome.

The ability of monitoring technology to advance in step with
weapons developments is dependent upon a willingness by political
authorities to see this as a crucial goal and spend the sums required.
One way in which regimes hostile to arms control can continue to cite
verification difficulties as a reason for delay is to fail to commit the
resources necessary to overcome such problems. It is noteworthy that
states tend to react to military challenges by building more weapons,
not by improving verification technologies to the point where such
weapons might be negotiated away. Such advances as have occurred
in verification technologies in the past 20 years have come about as a
by-product of efforts made to enhance general intelligence gathering
capabilities. In October 1979 the Senate Intelligence Committee
released an unclassified version of its findings on SALT II monitoring
capabilities and asked that 'arbitrary resource constraints' not be
allowed to hold back necessary improvements in American verification technologies. The committee recommended that a high budget
priority be given for 'processing and analysis, as well as for other
intelligence collection systems'.[40] The final phrase is a significant
one. The monitoring process does not produce too little information;
it produces too much in that there are not enough people available to
process and analyse the significance of all the information that is
being collected.

A curious feature of arguments about verification is that different criteria are used to judge the abilities of monitoring equipment depending on whether it is being used for treaty verification or for general intelligence gathering. As Stephen Meyer has noted, 'for some inexplicable reason there seems to be a widely held belief that monitoring capabilities that are not sufficient for arms control are somehow sufficient to guide "unconstrained" defence planning.'[41]

It can be argued that in practice the task of general intelligence gathering is less demanding than arms control verification because it is watching broad trends and overall force levels in traditional areas of such activity, whereas arms control monitoring requires precise measurements of exact numbers, and the need to ensure that forbidden activities are not happening anywhere.[42] Indeed arms control requirements, by giving the intelligence agencies more precise tasks, have led to improvements in responsiveness control and data management throughout the intelligence community.[43]

The different criteria seem to go beyond these 'tasking' explanations, however, leading to many paradoxes. The US public, for example, tends to become far more alarmed about debatable allegations of minor Soviet treaty non-compliance than it does about clear evidence of legal and unconstrained Soviet arms build-ups, even if the latter are on a massive scale.[44] Moreover, since the actual allegations themselves are based upon monitoring capabilities, those capabilities must have been deemed good enough to detect the minor infringements in order to enable the US to make the allegations of cheating; a circumstance which implies that confidence in monitoring abilities is actually higher than admitted.

A clear example of the discrepancy was given by Secretary of Defense Caspar Weinberger in 1983. Whereas the Pentagon made known that the mobility of the Soviet SS-20 would tax American monitoring capabilities so that a ban on INF in Europe could not be countenanced, a few days later Weinberger, seeking to stiffen European resolve to deploy cruise missiles, gave a precise count of SS-20 numbers, emphasizing the additional numbers deployed since an earlier report and noting that a further SS-20 deployment site was being prepared.[45]

Clearly, monitoring capabilities are better than is generally admitted. It would be surprising and reprehensible if this was not so since a state's own defence commitment and security will to a significant extent depend on its ability to gather accurate information about the other side's military inventory.

The truism that monitoring capabilities are crucial to progress in arms control tends to obscure the corollary that the technology of compliance monitoring can determine the scope of the actual agreements themselves. Ralph Earle, the chief US SALT II negotiator, declared that the US government 'formulated its proposal for the new agreement in terms of verifiable parameters'.[46] Using such criteria may well mean that arms control is being directed at systems which are comparatively easy to monitor, rather than at those systems which actually pose the greatest threat to strategic stability. Thus, for example, verification problems have meant that small mobile missiles have been banned to date, whereas from the point of view of long-term strategic stability they are far less dangerous than the large, multiple warhead, silo-based ICBMs which arms control agreements have favoured. Similarly, during the SALT II hearings Paul Nitze argued that the Carter administration had concentrated on limiting launchers rather than warheads because a warhead limit would have required increased cooperative verification methods.[47]

In 1981 the Reagan administration attempted to overcome this problem by announcing that it would no longer limit US arms control proposals to those that could be monitored by NTM but would devise 'substantive limitations that are strategically significant, and then construct the set of measures necessary to ensure verifiability'.[48] In practical terms this meant a greater emphasis on measures involving some form of OSI. For those who feel that data from NTM will become increasingly difficult to obtain, OSI offers a solution to the problem. In reality, however, the potential of OSI (except for certain specific instances such as a CTB) is of limited utility. OSI visitors, even those following up a challenge, would undoubtedly find no evidence of non-compliance. All such evidence would have been removed prior to their arrival. Nevertheless, as a confidence-building measure and as a useful addition to the 'multiple and duplicative methods of detection' mentioned earlier, OSI could play a useful role. It is not a panacea, however.

Given that OSI is often used as a challenge to Soviet seriousness on verification issues, it is worth at this point focusing specifically on the Soviet attitude towards arms control verification.

The Soviet Attitude Towards Verification

It is usually assumed that verification is overwhelmingly a Western concern, of little or no interest to the Soviet Union and its allies.[49] This view has been challenged recently, however, from both sides of the Iron Curtain. A Soviet journal in 1982 described progress in arms control and disarmament as hinging upon the verification issue,[50] while in 1984 the first book-length study of the question of verification from the Soviet perspective was published in the Soviet Union.[51] This too recognized the importance of the issue in a world divided ideologically, 'hence the need for special measures to ensure such compliance, in other words for verification of disarmament'.[52] Some Soviet commentators have even gone so far as to suggest that in fact verification monitoring is actually more important to the Soviet Union than it is to the NATO states, and particularly the US, on the grounds that the US has bases all round the periphery of the Soviet Union whereas the Soviet Union has no such analogous facilities (except for Cuba).[53] This is claiming too much, however. Because the US is an 'open' society it is much easier for the Soviet Union to verify US compliance with agreements than for the US when monitoring the Soviet Union.

The crucial point, however, is that although Soviet views and needs on this issue differ from those of the West, they still exist. It is not accurate to say that verification does not matter to the Soviet Union. The Soviet Union has no more reason to trust the US than vice versa. What is true is that the Soviet approach to verification differs markedly from that of the US.[54] This general attitude can be held to be true for the other WTO states since there have been no reported differences over the subject within WTO, as there have on other issues.[5]

The essence of the Soviet position is that monitoring of another state should be for the purpose of ensuring that agreed disarmament or arms control measures are in fact being fully implemented.[56] Any attempt to collect data on the Soviet Union's armed forces that is not directly relevant to an arms control agreement is seen by Moscow as espionage pure and simple.[57] Because of their traditional secretiveness the Soviets therefore are careful only to agree to verification which is clearly essential if a treaty desired by them is to be achieved.

They go to enormous lengths to define the verification clauses in such a way as to limit possible collateral intelligence gains by the West.

This is a perfectly reasonable and defensible position for the Soviet Union to adopt, but it inevitably causes problems. Apart from the fact that 'going the extra mile' on military transparency is a definite confidence-building measure, the Soviet attitude provides a fruitful seedbed for compliance disputes.

For example, in 1984 President Reagan charged that the Soviet Union was coding the telemetry from its missile tests in violation of Article XV of the SALT II treaty and that 'the nature and extent of encryption of telemetry on new ballistic missiles is an example of deliberate impeding of verification of compliance' of the agreement.[58] In fact not only does the SALT II treaty not forbid telemetry encryption, it specifically permits it under Article XV except when such encryption 'impedes verification of compliance with the provisions of the treaty'.[59] The treaty does not specify what telemetry is covered by this exception. After 1980 the US was particularly concerned about encryption of telemetry on tests of the SS-NX-20 SLBM, and the SS-X-25 ICBM. When the US protested about the encryption the Soviet Union replied that not all the coded information was covered by the SALT II limits, therefore if the US would identify which telemetry channels were the relevant ones, the Soviet Union would not encrypt them.[60]

This incident throws a great deal of light on Soviet verification attitudes. On the one hand, the Soviet attitude was legally correct in that the US had only to identify the relevant telemetry channels to obtain Soviet compliance as per SALT II. To this extent President Reagan's charge of 'deliberate cheating' was invalid. On the other hand, what the Soviets were doing was quite clearly a breach of faith in that no reasonable interpretation of SALT II could see it as allowing encryption of all test telemetry. By asking the US to name the channels relevant to the treaty (which the US refused to do), the Soviet Union was encouraging the US to reveal how good it was at reading Soviet missile telemetry. In other words the Soviets were not unreasonably trying to limit collateral US intelligence gains from SALT II, but they were doing it in such way that, if successful, the Soviet Union would benefit from collateral intelligence gains. This seemed another clear example of the Soviet attitude of 'what's mine is mine and what's yours is negotiable.'

The Soviet record on verification is full of such episodes. Overall the Soviet record is very good. Over a very large number of arms control agreements their compliance record is overwhelmingly positive. They have frequently gone to considerable lengths to clear up ambiguities or to resolve troublesome issues in ways beneficial to the West. Thus, for example, in 1976 the US became concerned that the Soviet Union was not dismantling old ICBM silos fast enough to stay within the 1972 SALT I limits as new strategic submarines were launched. Aware of this problem the Soviets acknowledged it even before the US formally complained and at their adversary's request delayed the sea-trials of a new SSBN for three months in order to stay within the limits.[61] The Soviet attitude in the Standing Consultative Committee set up by the SALT treaties has been constructive and positive.[62]

On the other hand, the Soviets have occasionally displayed an almost flippant lack of concern for Western interests on some issues which were bound to generate complaints and ill-feeling, as with the telemetry encryption. This schizophrenic behaviour is probably the result of the realities of the Kremlin world-view. The Soviet Union usually takes its treaty responsibilities very seriously indeed and invariably abides by its interpretation of the terms. It is important, therefore, for Western negotiators to make sure that the treaty terms are so drafted as to make Western and Soviet views of Soviet obligations concur because 'what you see is what you get.'

However, probably due to their political upbringing, not all Soviet leaders show an understanding for the realities of democratic politics in the West, where legal but mischievous Soviet behaviour affects the perceptions of politicians and public to the point where their continued support for arms control agreements may be seriously compromised.

Soviet attitudes towards verification are not static but have shown a steady evolution since 1945. Between 1945 and 1960 the Soviet Union tended to regard almost any from of monitoring as legalized espionage, a line it took in rejecting what it calls the 'notorious' Eisenhower Open Skies proposal of 1955. Indeed the Soviet Union has consistently argued that US monitoring proposals invariably 'go far beyond what is actually needed to ensure observance of concrete arms limitation and disarmament measures'.[63] Initially satellite reconnaissance was also seen in this light, but in 1963 this objection was abandoned in the context of the Partial Test Ban Treaty, and during the 1970s the USSR accepted as legitimate the verification of agreements using 'national technical means'. Thus, in the context of a report on Chairman Gorbachev's 1985 nuclear disarmament proposal, a Soviet journal noted that for the purposes of verification, 'existing national means of observation, including satellites and seismological, radar and other radioelectronic stations are highly effective.'[64]

Since 1970 in fact the Soviet Union has moved steadily towards a greater degree of military openness in the context of arms control agreements. For example, as part of the SALT II negotiations the Soviet Union released military data on its strategic nuclear forces for the first time, a move which (according to the chief Soviet negotiator Vladimir Semyenov) effectively 'repealed four hundred years of Russian history' of military secrecy.[65] Similar Soviet data release has occurred in the context of the MBFR and INF negotiations. The Soviets have also accepted the value of other 'cooperative measures', such as the agreement on the use of 'functionally related observable differences' to aid verification of SALT II, acceptance of the value of giving the US advance notice of its missile flight-tests and the importance of non-interference with the other side's national technical means of verification. The Soviet Union has offered to go beyond the 1986 Stockholm Agreement in extending confidence-building measures in Eastern Europe. In 1983 the Soviets announced that they would open up their civil nuclear reactors to inspectors from the International Atomic Energy Authority, an entirely voluntary concession. In January 1983 the WTO accepted the value of such 'international procedures' for compliance.[66]

Even on the highly sensitive issue of OSI the Soviet position has evolved dramatically. It has accepted a degree of OSI in two of the treaties it has signed, the TTBT and the PNET, and has proposed OSI in a number of its own arms control offers since 1980. Resistance to OSI is no longer a bench-mark of Soviet verification attitudes; the argument now is rather about how much OSI and of what kind, the principle having clearly been accepted.[67]

Indeed to some extent the boot is now on the other foot. The US has refused to ratify the TTBT and PNET even though these agreements embody the kind of OSI which the US says that the Soviet Union should accept, while in 1983 President Reagan's own Consolidated Verification Group rejected the idea of OSI on the grounds that it gave away too many secrets![68]

What has become clear since 1970 is that if the Soviet Union feels that an agreement is possible and would be in its interest, it accepts that because of western sensibilities the price of such an agreement may well be monitoring techniques which are fairly unpalatable. How much intrusiveness they will accept depends upon the nature of the negotiations and the value of the treaty to them. They may accept instrusive monitoring for technical or political reasons, but there are still clear limits as to how far they will go. Certainly they will continue to resist proposals which seem to them to simply hand out hunting licences for inspectors of Soviet military establishments.

Future flexibility will depend also on the general Soviet attitude to arms control. If the Soviets believe the US will not keep its side of the bargain, clearly they will be less inclined to make concessions on the verification issue and in this regard the US failure to ratify the TTBT of 1974, the PNET of 1976, and the 1979 SALT II Treaty, despite concessions made on verification, has given the Soviet Union good grounds for pessimism. The bitter arguments over Soviet compliance with earlier treaties is also bound to have some effect.

Compliance Diplomacy

One problem with arms control agreements is the question of what to do if the other side appears to be breaching the treaty. No treaty can be devised to cover every possible future contingency and therefore it is inevitable that compliance problems will arise from time to time. In his instructions to the SALT I negotiating team President Nixon declared that he was determined to avoid 'divisive disputes regarding Soviet compliance or non-compliance with an understanding or agreement. Nor will I bequeath to a future President the seeds of such disputes.'[69] In practice, however, just such disputes arose, and it would have been remarkable if they had not. Even after the treaty has been concluded, therefore, compliance diplomacy must be expected, which in effect will be a continuation of the negotiations.

Most disputes about compliance can be resolved relatively easily. Assuming that both sides continue to value the treaty then the source of the dispute is likely to reside either in ambiguous monitoring data, in which case additional information can be provided to clear up the problem, or in the two sides interpreting a treaty clause in different ways with both interpretations being reasonable. In the latter case some renewed bargaining will be necessary but a compromise should be possible which satisfies both parties. Problems of this sort can be kept to a minimum by avoiding treaty provisions which are difficult to monitor, but this may mean ignoring weapon developments which pose a serious risk to stability.

The real compliance difficulties arise when one side appears to be breaching the agreement, or a number of agreements, in a fairly systematic manner, thus raising serious doubts as to whether the other side values the agreement and is being seriously constrained by it.

Logically, in this latter situation the aggrieved party should withdraw from the treaty. In practice, however, the situation is rarely, if ever, this simple. For one thing, the evidence, while convincing to the government, may still be rather ambiguous so that national support for such a treaty withdrawal might clearly be lacking. Even assuming that the pattern of non-compliance is reasonably convincing the question arises of whether the adversary is still more constrained by being forced to act within the treaty, even with the apparent violations, than they would be if the treaty collapsed. If the answer to this question is affirmative then it may well be worth keeping complaints at a non-public level, or invoking sanctions that fall well short of withdrawal from the treaty.

A second reason for a restrained response could be a desire to protect intelligence sources. When monitoring treaty provisions it is wise to depend on two or more sources for each monitoring task. However, this is not always possible and a state detecting what appears to be an act of non-compliance may, if the non-compliance is small-scale, feel that it is more important to protect the source of the data than to draw attention to its monitoring capabilities by formally complaining about the alleged treaty violation.

The nature of the bargain represented by the treaty will also be a determining factor. If one side clearly got the best deal then it may see the treaty violations as the other side regaining a little of its lost ground, but with the balance of advantage still clearly in one's own favour. In this case once again it would make no sense to withdraw from a treaty so overwhelmingly favourable to oneself.

A further question that has to be asked is do these apparent violations actually matter? Given the difficulty of being absolutely certain, it would be of dubious value to abrogate a treaty on the grounds of allegations which, even if true, conferred little or no military advantage to the other side. As noted earlier the less likely that cheating will be detected, the more likely it is that such cheating would be militarily insignificant. Cheating of this order would also raise doubts about the data once again, since it is hardly likely that the other side would risk cheating (and being caught) for something that did not even give them a significant benefit; and neither is it likely that the other side would sign a treaty which forced them to cheat to protect their national security interests.[70]

The administrations of Presidents Nixon, Ford and Carter generally followed the logic of these arguments. They assumed that compliance disputes with the Soviet Union, which it was important for US security to resolve satisfactorily, did not mean that the Soviets were cheating; merely that their behaviour was not all that the US would wish. They sought to resolve compliance problems via mutual understandings and clearer, mutually acceptable definitions of ambiguous treaty clauses. They carefully avoided making accusations or indictments and opted for a 'fact-finding and problem-solving approach'.[71]

President Reagan, by contrast, preferred an accusatory approach. The different attitude was underpinned by a political rather than a military criterion for what constituted significant violations. The Nixon, Ford and Carter administrations adopted what has been termed a 'substantive' approach to arms control monitoring, arguing that a treaty could be adequately verified if neither side could alter the strategic balance by undetected cheating.[72] The Reagan approach, however, was 'legalistic', seeing violations as crucial regardless of their military insignificance.[73] The Reagan administration, unlike its predecessors, also made the *a priori* assumption that the Soviets would always cheat; therefore ambiguous data was evidence of guilt.

The 1984 US list of alleged Soviet compliance failures was thus a far from impressive document, reflecting a problem-creating rather than a problem-solving approach.[74] The charge of 'massive' Soviet violations was justified by assembling a long list of ambiguities and possible marginal violations with no regard for their relative insignificance and replete with caveats. Thus, for example, on the SS-16 missile the evidence was 'somewhat ambiguous' making a 'definite conclusion' impossible but it was deemed a 'probable violation' of

SALT II, while on the 150 kiloton test-limit the 'evidence was ambiguous', there were 'verification uncertainties' and thus the administration was 'unable to reach a definitive conclusion', but even so they estimated a 'likely violation' of SALT II.

Accusing a major state of cheating, when the evidence itself was so ambiguous, represented a dramatic diplomatic challenge by the US. In some ways the accusations might be deemed surprising since they came from an administration which deemed the treaties in question as 'fatally flawed', had no intention of ratifying them and insisted its compliance with their terms was a matter of chance rather than policy. One predictable effect of the accusations was sharply to reduce the chances of subsequent arms control accords, and this may well have been the main objective for those of the President's advisers who insisted on going public with the accusations. There is no doubt that by publicly airing such charges rather than pursuing the complaints through diplomatic channels the chances of a diplomatic solution were reduced because national pride and honour on both sides was put at stake.

Having gone public with the charges the Reagan administration then faced the crucial problem of how to respond to the alleged violations. Clearly the administration had to do something, since no state can be expected to continue to comply placidly with a treaty that, it has publicly argued, threatens its interests. The choice of response in such a situation is essentially between four courses of action. A government could activate 'hedging' programmes put on standby in anticipation of such a problem, as President Carter had warned he would do in such circumstances;[75] the administration could adopt a 'tit-for-tat' or 'proportionate' response; a third option would be to withdraw temporarily from parts of the treaty; or, finally, the US could withdraw from the relevant treaties altogether.

President Reagan chose the second option, with a public declaration that unless the complained-of behaviour ceased immediately the US would make proportionate breaches itself. In doing this, however, the US put its global image at risk. Since the evidence of Soviet cheating was by no means unambiguous, not everyone inside the US was convinced and there was deep scepticism among America's NATO allies, although on one or two issues (such as the Krasnoyarsk radar facility) they shared the concern of the US if not its conclusions.[76] Since verification is a subjective exercise – a matter of political, rather than technical judgement – the president's 'proportionate responses' ran the risk of being seen by others as unjustified unilateral treaty violations.[77]

Moreover, selective withdrawal runs the risk of undermining the entire treaty structure. Once this process is triggered by a collapse of confidence in the other side it is an extremely difficult process to reverse or even contain, since neither side will wish 'to be left at the starting gate when its negotiating partner pulls out of the agreements'.[78] In addition, proportionate response would mean effectively that the other side was not being punished, since equality of inconvenience was being maintained. To punish the other side it would really be necessary to respond by building up beyond the pre-treaty levels so that the treaty breaker would suffer a net loss.

A government sincerely committed to arms control has every right to expect the other side to abide by agreements and would be both justified and correct in announcing a willingness to 'punish' violations. However, a government that has made plain its disdain for arms control serves only to confirm its cynicism and substantiate its opponent's doubts by adopting such a policy.

Conclusions

Verification is a means to an end, not an end in itself; its purpose is to make arms control possible with safety rather than to block progress in this realm. If it is to achieve its purpose there must be, on the part of the monitoring states, a willingness to be reassured.[79] Ambrose Bierce defined peace as 'in international affairs, a period of cheating between two periods of fighting'.[80] This is an amusing *bon mot*, but it is not a basis for an arms control policy. It makes a considerable difference to the outcome of a verification exercise if the monitoring is expected to prove violation against an assumption of cheating.[81] Behaviour may be monitored which seems to be inconsistent with a treaty obligation, but it may not necessarily be a violation and governments must distinguish in this respect between 'behaviour it does not like and behaviour that is forbidden by treaties'.[82] Verification capabilities currently available, when taken in concert with careful treaty drafting, are more than adequate to sustain progress in arms control given the political willingness to pursue this goal. In the final analysis 'verifiability' must be a function of wide criteria for, as Stephen Meyer has noted, the ultimate question must be that of whether or not the risk involved in undetected cheating is greater than that involved in unconstrained arms racing.[83]

8

The Politics of Arms Control

Arms control is much more than two teams of negotiators glaring at each other across a bargaining table.

Kruzel, 'From Rush–Bagot to START: The Lessons of Arms Control[1]

Introduction

A judgement upon whether or not arms control has been a failure and what might be done to rejuvenate or reorient it needs to look at 'arms control' at two distinct levels: technical and political.

Throughout this book it has been emphasized that in its original formulation arms control was a far broader concept than the one which has subsequently gained public currency. On the one hand, arms control is a *technical* exercise, which can be pursued unilaterally, bilaterally or multilaterally and is designed to fine-tune the super-power nuclear balance so as to preserve deterrence and peace by eliminating incentives for one side to attack the other. On the other hand, arms control is a *political* exercise designed to demonstrate the desire of governments to reduce the scale and dangers of the nuclear confrontation by pursuing negotiated constraints and reductions in nuclear weapon systems.

It is clear from the record of the past 30 years that governments pursue both these forms of arms control, but not necessarily at the same time. When both are being pursued simultaneously government and public perceptions of the exercise as being valuable are likely to coincide. When the technical aspect is being pursued public opinion may be sceptical of the value of the exercise even though the outcome might be greater stability and a reduced risk of war. When the political aspect is being pursued public opinion may be supportive even if the eventual agreement makes little, if any, real contribution to stability and, indeed, may still be supportive even if no agreement results from the negotiations at all.

Has Arms Control been a Failure?

In the early 1980s arms control was subjected to sustained criticism from all quarters. Even supporters of the enterprise felt obliged to argue that arms control had failed, that 30 years of superpower negotiation had done little more than 'codify the arms race'.[2] To support this thesis the evidence of the SALT negotiations (1969–79) could be cited. During the period of the SALT I negotiations both sides pressed ahead with new deployments. It could be argued that SALT I represented a real 'brake' on this process, a 'cap' on the arms race. However, even after the cap was in place, the superpowers continued to modernize their strategic forces at a brisk pace. Between 1972 and 1979, the period between the two SALT treaties, the Soviet Union deployed three new ICBM types, the SS-17, SS-18 and SS-19, all of them MIRVed. In the same period it deployed two new SSBN types, each equipped with a new SLBM. Three new types of cruise missile were tested as well as the Blackjack strategic bomber. Warhead totals went up from around 2,800 at the time of SALT I to about 5,000 at the time of SALT II. If there was a cap on the arms race, it clearly did not fit very snugly.

The US was equally busy. Over the same period the Minuteman ICBM force was hardened and given a higher yield, more accurate warhead; the new MX ICBM was flight-tested and the B-52 bombers were modernized and given a new short-range nuclear missile. At the same time two new cruise missile types were flight-tested, the new B-1 bomber was developed and the 'stealth' strategic bomber programme was initiated. The improved Poseidon SSBNs were in turn superseded by the Trident submarine with the much more accurate and longer-range C-4 missile. The D-5 missile programme was also begun. With the steady MIRVing programme, force loadings rose from some 5,700 in 1972 to around 9,200 after SALT II. The 1970s were hardly 'a decade of neglect' for US strategic forces either.

To the proverbial disinterested observer, arms control seemed all arms and no control. Inevitably, perhaps, it conjured up the warning of John Stuart Mill: 'against a great evil, a small remedy does not produce a small result. It produces no result at all.' Whereas in the 1960s and early 1970s the pursuit of arms control was seen as a worthy and noble enterprise, by the beginning of the 1980s it had run into the sand, overwhelmed by intellectual and political exhaustion.

In a technical sense arms control had not, in fact, failed. Its original purpose was to stabilize the deterrent balance, and by the mid-1970s a stable balance had been achieved; indeed, the very stability of that balance tended to reduce the will to pursue arms control in the political sense. The strategic balance was not seen as being so threatened as to require urgent measures to buttress it. The exception that proved the rule to this was the threat of nationwide ABM defences in the late 1960s which led to the ABM Treaty of 1972. The balance was maintained at very high levels of weaponry, it is true, but that very fact made it impervious to sudden threats. Because deterrence was actually more secure than either the opponents or supporters of arms control generally argued, the situation arose in which the superpowers deemed it necessary to enter into arms control negotiations, but did not feel obliged to conclude arms control agreements.

The stability of the deterrent balance in the late 1970s was a result of arms control, but arms control in the terms of the original formulators of the concept: that is, embracing unilateral force improvement measures as well as international agreements. The balance that emerged was not so much a result of negotiation as the product of an historical convergence of aggregate superpower strategic force levels. The US built up to a predetermined level and when the Soviet Union reached approximate equality the two sides relaxed their efforts, ratifying this decision in the SALT I agreement. Subsequent 'competition' involved qualitative improvements rather than increases in the numbers of launchers.

The process proved more durable than some feared in 1981 because agreements like SALT II did little more than ratify unilateral defence programmes. The SALT regime did not rapidly collapse when the Reagan administration assumed office, but this was because the treaty allowed the US to do everything it wanted in the next six years anyway. Since it involved no real constraints there was no urgent need to reject it. Reagan administration officials in fact argued that this was the only legitimate function of arms control; that it was only useful when it confined itself to 'registering and codifying an existing balance of forces'.[4]

If the 'technical' arms control approach is being pursued, this makes good sense. Given that the current offence-dominant balance at high levels of weaponry is extremely stable, an arms control approach limited to ratifying unilateral force improvements within broad parameters would help sustain that stability. The ability of each side to plan its force programmes with high confidence in the intelligence estimates of the adversary's future force structure could also gain greatly from the existence of a stable arms control regime.

However, while such a regime satisfies the technical criteria for success in arms control it does not satisfy the political criteria. For the latter, movement towards reduction in weapon inventories is the key factor. However, reductions have been very hard to deliver. States seem to feel more comfortable protecting their own weapon programmes, rather than reducing those of potential adversaries. Given that the strategic situation is *currently* extremely stable and that governments are hesitant regarding the implications of significant reductions, it is a moot point whether arms control negotiations have contributed anything in the past or would do so in the future. In other words, is arms control really necessary?

Is Arms Control Necessary?

Senator Joseph Biden, a supporter of arms control, remarked in late 1986 that, 'the past six years have demonstrated that the world can survive in the short term without progress in nuclear arms control.'[5] In part this stems from the forces making arms control possible in the first place. One of the ironies of arms control is that it is made possible by improved relations rather than being a precursor to such improvements. As Kruzel has noted, states verging on the conclusion of an agreement make clear their real judgement about the likelihood of conflict. 'This is the Catch-22 of arms control; by the time nations find themselves able to conclude an agreement they may not need to do so.'[6] Thus a period of negotiation is likely to be followed by one of comparatively little change so long as the objective realities which led to the negotiations continue to remain relevant.

The belief that arms control in fact has had comparatively little impact, either positive or negative, is widely held. Agreements tend to ratify parity, rather than create it. Treaties such as the Limited Test Ban Treaty of 1963 occurred in a climate of improving superpower relations following the 1962 Cuban Missile Crisis. The agreement reflected a better relationship but it did not create one.[7] This is a general tendency. It is only in an improving international atmosphere that increases in trust between nations take place, thereby facilitating arms control. Arms control agreements are often visible symbols of an improved relationship and are occasionally sought for just this reason, as with the Reagan–Gorbachev INF treaty of 1987.

Scepticism has also been expressed as to whether arms control can achieve one of its other set goals, namely that of reducing the death and destruction involved should war occur. Such an outcome would only be possible if the war was terminated within a few months. When a war breaks out, war stocks are rapidly exhausted and are then replaced with new production and purchases, with both these occurring on a far higher scale than in peacetime.[8] Once war breaks out arms control has little, if any, role to play.

A further caveat regarding the value of arms control is that it may sometimes act as a barrier to the attainment of its own objectives. Thus, for example, over the past quarter of a century the superpowers have been steadily replacing their huge and fantastically destructive nuclear weapons with much smaller-yield devices. This has only been possible due to a continuous process of warhead refinement which would have been impossible if a CTB had been in place.

It can be argued, therefore, that the world can cope without the necessity for ponderous arms control negotiations which rarely achieve the stated aims of arms control advocates and certainly never do so without imposing all sorts of costs in terms of displacement effects. However, the value of the arms control process should not be judged simply, or even primarily, in terms of the agreements arrived at. The real value of arms control is political, rather than technical, and its pursuit generates a variety of benefits which are not always immediately obvious.

Arms control is part of national security policy. Its purpose is to produce security for states by pursuing cooperative efforts with potential adversaries, even while unilateral force improvements are

being undertaken as a complementary route to national security. As
it has developed since 1960 arms control has come to play a crucial
role in legitimizing such unilateral improvements and in defining
their limits. In the absence of serious efforts to negotiate arms
control, administrations encounter greater difficulty in sustaining a
national consensus behind prudent and realistic defence efforts.
Opponents of heavy defence expenditure withdraw their political
support, while supporters attempt to recreate a consensus by playing
up images of the adversary which are a distortion of reality. Hostile
image creation of this sort is neither sensible in itself in the nuclear
age, nor is it conducive to producing defence efforts geared towards
objective reality. It is more likely to trigger offsetting reactions from
the adversary and produce an increase in arms racing, with no gain to
either side.

In contrast, pursuing necessary defence programmes in tandem
with arms control reassures the public that while the necessary
defence effort is being maintained, everthing possible is being done to
reduce the scale of the effort required to match the adversary,
resulting in savings for both sides without loss of security. As well as
the economic burden involved, the public tends to feel that
unrestrained arms races increase the risk of confrontation and war. A
government which scorns arms control whilst accelerating defence
expenditures is likely to forfeit public trust and risk losing support for
objectively essential defence programmes. President Reagan had this
danger clearly in mind during the 1984 presidential election when he
continually stressed his commitment to achieving arms control agreements in his second term. Unfortunately, the public seem satisfied
with the mere appearance of effort. Incumbent administrations are
not punished electorally if they fail to produce agreements so long as
they can convince the electorate that they have been honestly
endeavouring to reach such agreements and that the failure to do so
lies more with the adversary than themselves.

Earlier chapters of this book have looked at the very real difficulties
involved in arms control negotiations. Failure is not always due to
lack of a desire to succeed in the first place. When the parties involved
wrestle with the complexities in a sincere manner they signal to a
watching world that they recognize the fact that their armaments
alarm others and that they are seeking to demonstrate their lack of
aggressive intent. This is crucial in reassuring both their adversaries

and their own populations that the weaponry is for deterrent purposes only. In this sense 'armaments are about deterrence and arms control about reassurance. Security is achieved by a synthesis of the two.'[9] The role of arms control is to ensure that a potential adversary will not be driven to war through a misperception of the other side's intentions, and neither will domestic support for a strong defence be undermined by a similar misperception of these same intentions.

The existence of arms control demonstrates to an occasionally nervous public that there are, in fact, very real limits to the military competition between the superpowers which neither is eager to go beyond. If the process is rather pedestrian and rarely exciting, it is no less vital for being 'an ornament of civilisation that adorns an otherwise brutal struggle'.[10] Neither should it be thought that simply because arms control is somewhat ritualistic and limited in its impact it is not a great cause, for it is; and, as Michael Howard has noted, it is exactly the international rivalries, hatreds and suspicions which make arms control so complex and difficult to achieve that also make it so necessary.[11]

Goals and Mechanisms

If arms control is an object worth pursuing, it needs to be pursued in new ways, both in terms of the mechanisms deemed appropriate and in terms of its fundamental objectives. In its original formulation arms control was seen as a method for helping to sustain the strategic balance between the superpowers by constraining competition and anticipating and foreclosing threats to strategic stability. Arms control was the handmaiden of the theory of strategic deterrence and it is in terms of the technical requirements of deterrence theory that the US has pursued arms control. Increasingly, however, the refinements of deterrence have hindered the attainment of the political objectives arms control is seen to serve, and it is by no means obvious that in this conflict of interests the arcane desiderata of deterrence theory should be encouraged to prevail. To date neither superpower has fully accepted the major constraints implied in deterrence theory: that is, that neither should pursue wholly effective defences or a disarming first-strike capability. At the same time the alleged requirements for effective deterrence have been steadily refined, driven by the belief that if a threat is conceivable it must be assumed to exist and be catered for. In addition, while the 'threat' is usually defined in terms of capability and intent, the intent element in the equation is deemed irrelevant in the sense that a willingness to use the capability in certain circumstances is assumed.

Thus while in the literature of strategic theory deterrence and arms control are closely intertwined, in practice the two pull in quite different directions since they are based upon different assumptions. Arms control implies that the common value of mutual survival in the nuclear age supersedes lesser national interests and creates a compelling requirement for limited competition, clear communication of non-aggressive intention, and mutual pursuit of negotiated arms constraints. Deterrence, in contrast, while sharing the goal of avoidance of nuclear war, creates a requirement for ever more numerous and more varied nuclear weapon stockpiles to ensure that deterrence can be sustained at all times under all conceivable scenarios. Likewise it generates a requirement for deeply xenophobic imagery since the adversary's population is to be continuously threatened with genocide by incineration and radiation, a posture so clearly immoral that only the assumption of evil in the 'target' population could justify it; that, and the fact that the threat is daily reciprocated by the other side.

Deterrence, in the form of Mutually Assured Destruction, is held to produce greater security by creating absolute insecurity. The arms control concept, by contrast, assumes that there is no such thing as complete security in the nuclear age because one side's security is purchased at the price of the other's. The only security objectives which are rational, therefore, are those which optimize both sides' security and these can only be pursued effectively in a cooperative framework.

There is a further mismatch encouraged by deterrence theory. Arms controllers have long argued that arms control and disarmament require a degree of trust between the two sides and that successive agreements enhance that trust, making further agreements possible. However, it is not easy to sustain this belief when the objective reality is a pattern of continuing strategic deployments at ever-higher levels. The experience of the 1970s showed that the public become disenchanted with arms control if the other side are deploying new weapons despite the agreements, notwithstanding that the new deployments are quite permissible under the terms of the agreement.

Public perceptions of threat in the mid-1970s moved back into line with the apparent message of the weapon deployments, rather than that contained in the arms control agreements. [12]

In order to create a total consensus on security and arms control goals a reformulation of the requirements of deterrence is therefore needed. This would have to embrace the elimination of the more bizarre scenarios from the threat assessment and a modification of the target coverage utilized in the SIOP. Only by reducing the requirements for maintained deterrence could the path be opened for the kind of deep, sustained reductions in nuclear inventories called for by both superpower leaders at the 1986 Reykjavik summit. Reductions are now so clearly associated in the public mind with effective arms control that their low priority in early arms control thought is now irrelevant. They have become a kind of optical measurement for arms control progress. Without a reassessment of deterrence requirements, warhead reductions would cease with both sides still maintaining more than 6,000 strategic nuclear warheads, the minimum number needed to meet their current target coverage requirements.

Visible reductions are needed for other reasons as well. Irrespective of the objective reality of superpower relations, the existence of grossly inflated nuclear arsenals will always create its own reality, undermining trust and sustaining fear. Nuclear weapons will not be eliminated overnight, and indeed there are cogent reasons for arguing that they should not be totally eliminated even if it were possible, but gradual reductions from the current massive totals are necessary to counter the illusion that because each side possesses such weapons one or both must harbour the desire to annihilate the other: an idea that is patent nonsense.

A major obstacle to the attainment of arms control at present is the absence of a clear view of the strategic environment that it is expected to underpin. Agreements are designed to sustain or facilitate a desired strategic environment. They cannot do this if there is uncertainty or disagreement over the environment that is desirable. This is why SDI has become a major stumbling block to progress in strategic arms control. If one side wants to promote defence-dominance and the other does not, agreements become tremendously difficult to formulate. In an offence-dominant world, for example, the Soviet Union seems prepared to countenance deep cuts in the nuclear stockpile because mutual vulnerability would continue to exist even at much lower arms levels. In a world of strategic defences, however, this calculation changes because more warheads are required to allow for losses to the ⌐efences and thus the incentive to reduce is weakened; indeed, an incentive to increase the number of warheads is created.

Arms controllers have remained suspicious of SDI not only because the ABM Treaty remains one of the few effective ratified agreements the superpowers have signed, but also because by agreeing to leave themselves mutually vulnerable the two sides reinforced powerful incentives to cooperate in reducing the dangers inherent in the mutual hostage relationship. Crisis management was crucially important when both lay open to nuclear devastation. The 'cult of the defensive', by contrast, threatened to leave one side with a much reduced fear of retaliation and therefore less incentive to cooperate or to limit competition where it runs the risk of escalating into war.

The breaking of the 'linkage' between SDI and progress in other arms control areas in 1986 was a crucial development. It meant that while talks on strategic nuclear reductions remained deadlocked, progress could be made in other areas. The immediate effect of this was to open the way for a treaty eliminating the missile element of the INF of NATO, and the WTO. This was essential because by 1987 the arms control approach was in desperate need of some visible sign of progress to demonstrate that it had not totally failed.

The breakthrough was interesting in a number of ways. It appeared to validate those like Leslie Gelb who had argued that superpower arms control should 'be fashioned to move in small steps to do what can be done and to reach agreement expeditiously'. [13] The 'displacement effect' was rapidly apparent, however, with NATO giving immediate thought to ways of offsetting the lost nuclear capability with new nuclear deployments. [14] Because such deployments would be additional increments to existing forces they would be paradoxical in a number of ways. For one thing, their military utility would be seriously open to question. Certainly they would possess none of the advantages of the systems they were replacing. Second, an outcome which left overall warhead numbers almost unchanged would still produce the desired improvement in popular morale and international relations since the high-profile INF systems would be removed and their replacements would be virtually unnoticed by the concerned public. A few extra bombers or bombs deployed would not affect the impact of images of the withdrawal of cruise launchers from

Greenham Common, for example. In arms control it is not so much overall numbers which make an impression upon public perceptions, but rather the impression of movement in either direction and progress or lack of it at the negotiations.

The second significant feature of the 1987 INF negotiations was that because the Soviet Union had made a series of concessions, agreeing to each new NATO disarmament demand in turn, NATO was forced into a long overdue reassessment of what exactly it wanted from the arms control process. Most of the time all it wants is the negotiations themselves, and whether they lead to an agreement or not is a secondary consideration. However, once the Soviet Union made it clear that it was prepared to countenance significant reductions and even the total elimination of entire categories of nuclear weapons, then the question had to be faced. Did NATO actually want significant nuclear disarmament of this kind?

The answer to this question was no. NATO is not interested in complete nuclear disarmament and, moreover, never has been. From its inception NATO has been a nuclear alliance, committed to strategies based upon the threatened use of nuclear weapons. There are two reasons for this. The first, which is commonly cited, is that the Warsaw Pact enjoys a significant advantage in the size of its conventional forces over NATO on the crucial central front. Since the NATO members are not prepared to spend the money required to match the WTO, by default NATO has been thrown back upon the nuclear deterrent as a way of off setting the WTO conventional advantage.

This explanation has only ever been part of the picture, however. It has always begged the question of why, when the USA and Western Europe both have GNPs twice that of the Soviet Union, giving NATO a 4:1 advantage, and given that the WTO advantage has never been an unbridgeable gap, have the NATO states not made the comparatively modest effort required to close the gap?

The real reason is that NATO does not particularly want to close the gap. Certainly it wants the WTO conventional advantage kept within the margin of safety and would negotiate a balance if it could, but the issue is not a crucial one. It is not crucial precisely because NATO believes in the deterrent utility of nuclear weapons. NATO keeps its nuclear arsenal not because it is cheap, but because it is believed to *work*. NATO would not want a denuclearized Europe or denuclearized world even if such a goal were attainable. Conventional balances of power have not historically guaranteed peace. The nuclear balance, by contrast, has seen a continuous peace in Europe. It can be argued that the existence of NATO's nuclear arsenal may not have been the only, or indeed the most important, factor in the long peace in Europe since 1945, but in the absence of clear evidence to the contrary, NATO chooses to believe that it was. Because of this there has always been an inconsistency between NATO's strategy and its professed long-term disarmament goals. As long as very little disarmament was taking place this did not matter. The flurry of Soviet arms control concessions in 1987 caused this assumption to be reassessed, however. NATO felt obliged to state publicly for the first time that while it favoured major reductions in the nuclear stockpiles of the alliances, there was a point beyond which it was not prepared to go and that point was a long way short of total denuclearization.[15] NATO favours reductions, but opposes abolition of nuclear weapons.

This enunciation of its real arms control goals was long overdue. It had the effect of bringing the contemporary pursuit of nuclear arms control more in line with the anti-abolitionist views of the 1950s arms control community. It also made it possible for Western publics to comprehend exactly what was on offer and what was not, and to judge agreements against realistic alternatives, rather than against idealistic outcomes that were never remotely in prospect. Arms control is an activity which, even when successful, can only bring about small gains in security. It is politically unwise to encourage a popular belief that massive disarmament is potentially only one set of negotiations away from realization. It is unwise not only because the goal is unattainable while making actual agreements seem poor by comparison, but also because it encourages the belief that the current situation is intolerably dangerous and that a large dose of disarmament would *inevitably* lead to a more peaceful world. This is not necessarily true; indeed, it is one of the ironies of the times that those who oppose existing security relationships are said to belong to the 'peace movement' even though the existing system has produced over four decades of peace, while a change in the system might trigger instability and war. This is not to argue that the current situation is ideal, merely that it has worked so far. The desire to improve it stems not from its failures to date, but rather from a fear that the conditions which have underpinned it for so long are unlikely to last forever.

Ironically, one of the catalysts in undermining the consensus in favour of nuclear deterrence was President Reagan, author of an unprecedented military build-up during his period in office. By calling for SDI to render nuclear weapons 'impotent and obsolete', Reagan both cut away the moral props of nuclear deterrence theory and triggered for the first time serious discussion among the Western strategic community of what a world in which offensive nuclear weapons were not dominant might be like.

With the emergence in Mikhail Gorbachev of a Soviet leader seemingly committed to the same goal, a threshold has been crossed. Gerard Smith, head of the US SALT I negotiating team, has quoted Jean Monnet's belief that: 'It was important for the negotiating parties to consider themselves on one side of the table with the problem on the other – with the negotiators acting not as adversaries but as people trying to solve problems together.'[16]

What was significant about the Reagan–Gorbachev dialogue was the manner in which nuclear weapons were clearly defined as being part of the problem rather than part of the solution. Arms control tends to stress the former, deterrence theory the latter. President Reagan himself argued that the problem should be addressed by developing the capability to defend against nuclear weapons. Subsequent administrations, following Reagan's own nuclear critique, are likely to give greater weight to negotiating significant reductions in warhead levels rather than maintaining the warheads and developing expensive techniques for shooting them down.

There is a potential dilemma here for Western arms controllers. The Reagan–Gorbachev dialogue has led NATO to look at two different and conflicting future arms control routes. On the one hand, there is the US-led critique of nuclear deterrence and the search for political or technical means to lift the nuclear sword of Damocles. On the other hand is the European-favoured approach: nuclear disarmament should be pursued but only as far as low levels of deployment, not to the point of abolition. In the long term these two outlooks will be very difficult to reconcile. The long term is still at least decades away, however.

A further change in attitudes which accelerated during the 1980s was the crucial broadening of the concept of confidence- and security-building measures. One of Mikhail Gorbachev's criticisms of the US position at Reykjavik was that 'The scope of our partner's approach, was not broad enough.'[17] Gorbachev also called for bold, innovative solutions' and criticized those who always look to the past for guidance. This last criticism is interesting in that it is a criticism more of previous Soviet approaches than of Western ones. It is the Soviet Union which has traditionally preferred cautious, structured, incremental progress in arms control. There is, in fact, a great deal to be said for this approach, and had SALT III followed SALT II by the end of Ronald Reagan's first four years in office, the Soviet strategic nuclear force would have been 20 per cent smaller than it was in the absence of these agreements. However, the ponderous incremental approach does suffer from the fact that the pace of technological change leaves it struggling to keep up. The more innovative approach called for by Gorbachev offers the prospect of the kind of radical arms control agreements which could have a profound impact upon the size of the nuclear armouries, and the international images those armouries tend to sustain.

Gorbachev's first point, that a broader approach is required, was perfectly true but this was something that the West had long since realized. The arms control approach has to date been applied in a mechanistic fashion. This may have been because many of the founding fathers of arms control were mathematicians and economists rather than political scientists. They lacked a feel for political realities as compared to mathematical constructions. There is an old adage which argues that 'weapons do not kill people, people kill people.' There is a fundamental reality in this. The fact that Norway and Sweden have armed forces does not lead the two states to live in fear of each other, each waiting for the moment to strike when the other is weakest, or when it senses its own power beginning to fail. Yet this is the situation which is supposed to prevail between the superpowers. The crucial difference is not the presence of weapons which exist in both cases, but rather the attitudes and assumptions about the nature of the political relationship between the two countries. Nuclear arms control, if it addresses itself merely to the limitation of the weapon systems deployed by each side, misses the essential point. The real problem to be addressed is that of avoiding nuclear war, and in achieving this the nature of the political rivalry between the superpowers and the dangers of misperception stemming from the secretive nature of military activities are at least as important, if not more important, than the maintenance of a crude balance of destructive capability.

The Soviet Union, of course, has always stressed the importance of political realities as against hardware balances, but under Gorbachev it appears to have moved significantly closer towards understanding the basis of NATO's feelings of insecurity, and to have accepted that in the nuclear era Soviet (and indeed Russian) military and political traditions will have to be questioned if greater security is to be achieved. *Bezopasnost*, the absence of danger, is an impossibility and 'any nation which strives for absolute security inevitably creates dangers for other nations.'[18] If this is true as regards the dangers of America's SDI, which it is, it is equally true regarding the dangers created by the closed nature of Soviet society which makes arms control verification more difficult and encourages worst-case analysis in Western intelligence communities.

If neither side desires to attack the other, as both claim, then both must demonstrate this through greater military transparency and a greater willingness to concede some of the military advantages of secrecy in favour of the political advantages of openness. This means a profound change of attitude for both sides, abandoning the narrow pursuit of comparative advantage in favour of an approach which attempts to understand the other side's needs and outlook and searches for the points of agreement in each side's proposals, building upon these. It means also the conscious acceptance of the need for self-restraint, avoiding the understandable temptation to exploit and expand the adversary's problems whenever possible.

Gorbachev himself has taken important steps to educate the Soviet Party and population in the new realities of the nuclear age, telling the 27th Party Congress in 1986 that:

> In the context of the relations between the USSR and the USA, security can only be mutual, and if we take international relations as a whole it can only be universal. The highest wisdom is not in caring exclusively for oneself, especially to the detriment of the other side. It is vital that all should feel equally secure, for the fears and anxieties of the nuclear age generate unpredictability in politics and concrete actions.[19]

Even more significantly, perhaps, Gorbachev has argued that the ideological contest must take account of nuclear realities. His argument that the confrontation with capitalism can only take peaceful forms is not new (Khrushchev said the same thing 30 years earlier), but Gorbachev has gone further and echoed John F. Kennedy's view: the purpose of arms control in the nuclear age is to make the world safe for diversity. In August 1986 he told Soviet television viewers that the time had passed when either superpower could try to force other states to choose a political path, whether socialist or capitalist, and that each state must 'determine its social development autonomously'.[20]

For an ideological state like the Soviet Union these views are revolutionary, but they correctly reflect the reality that with nuclear-armed superpowers the central task is to find the political means to avoid developments which run the risk of escalating into war.

Once again, therefore, reductions as such are a less vital goal than changing the nature of the competition. Reductions are worth achieving because the size of the current stockpiles has a negative impact upon each side's images of the other, but arms control cannot have any meaningful impact upon the destructive impact of a nuclear war for decades to come. The levels of overkill are too great for this, though movement in the desired direction is to be welcomed. The US political system cannot cope with several sets of negotiations simultaneously and needs clear priorities, and the best route forward would be one that focused on manageable categories and used the limited political capital available to seek tangible ways to enhance each side's confidence in the good intentions of the other, rather than pursuing token reductions, or worse, 'mindless force matching and obsessions with the most irrelevant asymmetries'.[21] As long as the nature of the political confrontation remains essentially unchanged, then the potential of arms control will remain limited.

Bearing in mind that the impact of nuclear weaponry upon the nature of international relations is likely to change only slowly, Johan Holst has put forward the idea of a permanent superpower 'seminar on strategy' in which each side would present the rationale for its new weapon programmes, allowing the other to raise questions and debate the implications of the proposed programmes.[22] This would be a valuable exercise, allowing a broader scope of debate than that generated by the specific issues in particular negotiations. Arms control is in any case essentially 'an intellectual effort to anticipate and avoid the most dangerous aspects of a military competition',[23] and it is easier to achieve constraint prior to deployment than subsequently. However, the 1979 experience, when NATO offered not to deploy

Cruise and Pershing if the WTO scrapped its SS-4s, SS-5s and SS-20s, was not encouraging. The WTO refused and it took a further eight years of political furore, poisoned international relations and expensive deployments before an agreement was reached which was virtually identical to the 1979 NATO offer. Even so, with this bitter object lesson and a more astute and flexible Soviet leadership in Moscow, there is a lot to be said for reviving the philosophy behind the 1979 offer, which is that of Holst's seminar on strategy; deployments should not occur if the threat that is their rationale can be eliminated through negotiation, and if they do occur the other side will at least clearly understand the thinking behind them. Arms control is essentially a political, rather than a military, exercise and it cannot be isolated from the political realities of the prevailing domestic and international context. Its central purpose is to promote stability and to enhance confidence, and in this regard it is as important to address the 'software' of deployment patterns, warnings of exercises and a general openness in military preparations, as it is to deal with the 'hardware', the actual weapons themselves.

Conclusions

Arms control has not been a failure. Judged in terms of its original objectives, to create a more stable nuclear balance and by so doing to avert war, it has been a complete success. There has been no superpower nuclear war (an achievement which should not simply be taken for granted as if no other outcome was possible), the strategic nuclear balance is far more stable than it was 30 years ago, and the danger of war has greatly receded. It was the very success of this nuclear stability which robbed arms control efforts of real drive in the 1970s when both sides were reasonably content with the balance and therefore adopted a cautious and conservative approach at the negotiations. However, it has achieved the primary objective set for it by its original proponents.

Where arms control has failed has been in the political realm. Its mechanistic, incremental approach has left it victim to signal failures such as the inability to prevent the multiple-warhead revolution of the 1970s and, in a more general sense, the willingness to tolerate balances at steadily higher levels has produced a public loss of faith in arms control and a loss of self-belief among the arms control community.

The complexities of the arms control process, outlined in earlier chapters, suggest very clearly the need for a reassessment of the purpose and methods of arms control. In terms of purpose the goals have not altered; continuing strategic stability structured in such a way as to rule out the possibility of a successful nuclear attack by one superpower upon the other remains the central objective. All other objectives, whether saving money, reducing the damage of conflict and so on, must remain subordinate to the goal of preventing the outbreak of war in the first place.

In terms of methods, however, there is a clear need for change and considerable evidence that the necessary changes are likely to take place. The goal of achieving stability at lower rather than higher levels of deployment has become part of the arms control canon. There is a new commitment on both sides to radical but genuine proposals. Radical reductions have a far greater military and political impact than do marginal reductions and, moreover, they enable many of the inherent complexities of the arms control process to be sidestepped. In terms of verification, for example, it is easier to spot the existence of something where there should be nothing than it is to spot a 466th warhead where there should only be 465. Radical reductions also meet the criteria of satisfying a sceptical public that all the diplomatic effort is actually achieving something. In adopting zero in Europe as the goal for reductions of INF missiles, the superpowers accepted this logic. The greater Soviet willingness to accept major reductions as a genuine negotiating goal opens the way for significantly greater success in the 1990s than arms control saw in the 1980s.

Some important reservations need to be made, however. In the first place, whatever the public might think, reductions are not always the most fruitful goal to pursue. The world will be safer if certain weapons are retained but deployed in secure, visible and non-threatening ways than if the weapons were totally removed. Agreements such as the 1986 Stockholm Agreement on confidence- and security-building measures will sometimes be of more value than reductions *per se*.

A second caveat is that there are risks associated with nuclear reductions aimed at zero deployments. This can be seen clearly in the

European context. If NATO genuinely believes that the conventional imbalance requires nuclear deployments, then an expensive NATO conventional build-up, perhaps coupled with an arms control agreement in which the WTO made proportionately greater reductions, could create a conventional balance which would make possible nuclear disarmament.

In this situation the danger of war would increase, precisely because the risk of nuclear weapons being employed had been eliminated. However, total denuclearization of this sort would require the kind of intensive verification which it is impossible to conceive of any Western state accepting, still less a Communist state. To avert the danger of a conventional conflict, equally stringent verification of massively constraining conventional confidence-building measures would also be required. These prerequisites are not likely to be met in the foreseeable future.

An alternative scenario might suggest a technical way out of the nuclear dilemma. President Reagan's SDI was designed to render nuclear weapons 'impotent and obsolete'. However, the technical difficulties associated with an effective BMD, the variety of options open to the attacker, and the fact that the offence–defence struggle is always dynamic means that both sides would be likely to retain offensive forces even if they chose to deploy nationwide defences.

The outlook, therefore, is for a balance of power that will continue to be underpinned by the existence on both sides of numerous and diverse offensive nuclear systems. The 1990s are likely to see far more arms control agreements than the 1980s, and these agreements are likely to be far more radical than those of the 1970s, but they will not lead to anything remotely resembling 'denuclearization'. Arms control's purpose will continue to be what it has been for the past 30 years: to contain the superpower competition within stable limits in order to buy time for the advance of technology and political wisdom in an attempt to enable the construction of stable security relationships built upon less dangerous foundations than the current nuclear deterrent.

Notes

Chapter 1   The Origins of Arms Control

1 Thomas C. Schelling and Morton H. Halperin, *Strategy and Arms Control* (New York, 1961), p. 142.
2 William R. Frye, 'The Quest for Disarmament since World War Two', in Louis Henkin (ed.), *Arms Control: Issues for the Public* (Englewood Cliffs, New Jersey, 1961), p. 23.
3 William R. Frye, 'Characteristics of Recent Arms Control Proposals and Agreements', in Donald G. Brennan (ed.), *Arms Control, Disarmament and National Security* (New York, 1961), pp. 73-4. A book often called the 'Bible' of arms control.
4 Bernard G. Bechhoefer, *Postwar Negotiations for Arms Control* (Washington, DC, 1961), p. 562.
5 Frye 'Characteristics', p. 75.
6 Bechhoefer, *Postwar Negotiations*, p. 565.
7 Robert R. Bowie, 'Basic Requirements of Arms Control', in Brennan, *Arms Control*, p. 43.
8 Schelling and Halperin, *Strategy*, p. 142.
9 Ibid., p. 142.
10 Thomas C. Schelling, 'Reciprocal Measures for Arms Stabilisation', in Brennan, *Arms Control*, p. 167.
11 The European-American Assembly, 'Defence, Disarmament and the Free World', in Ernest W. Lefever (ed.), *Arms and Arms Control* (New York, 1962), p. 122.
12 Schelling and Halperin, *Strategy*, p. 143.
13 Hedley Bull, *The Control of the Arms Race* (London, 1961), p. 8.
14 James E. King, Jr, 'Arms Control and United States Security', in Henkin, *Arms Control*, p. 111.

15 Jerome B. Weisner, Foreword to Brennan, *Arms Control*, p. 14.

16 John W. Spanier and Joseph L. Nogee, *The Politics of Disarmament:* in *Soviet-American Gamesmanship* (New York, 1962), p. 11.

17 Ibid., p. 15.

18 Bernard T. Feld, 'Inspection Techniques of Arms Control', in Brennan, *Arms Control*, p. 320. See also Brennan's preface, p. 9. Both Schelling and Halperin, *Strategy*, pp. 2–3 and Bull, *Control of the Arms Race*, p. ix, argued that arms control was not so much an alternative to disarmament as a broader concept which could encompass disarmament as one possible approach.

19 Bull, *Control of the Arms Race*, p. 61.

20 Jerome B. Weisner, 'Comprehensive Arms Limitation Systems', in Brennan, *Arms Control*, p. 198.

21 Schelling, 'Reciprocal Measures', p. 168.

22 Robert R. Bowie, 'Arms Control and United States Foreign policy', in Henkin, *Arms Control*, p. 75.

23 For example, Arnold Wolfers, Paul H. Nitze and James E. King, Jr, 'Arms Control and Other Approaches to Stability,' in Lefever, *Arms*, p. 8.

24 Schelling and Halperin, *Strategy*, p. 57.

25 For example, Henkin, who wrote interchangeably of the traditional 'disarmament' and the modern phrase 'arms control'. Henkin, *Arms Control*, p. 4.

26 Spanier and Nogee, *Politics of Disarmament*, p. 15.

27 Weisner, 'Arms Limitation', p. 204.

28 Bull, *Control of the Arms Race*, p. 10.

29 Donald G. Brennan, 'Setting and Goals of Arms Control', in Brennan, *Arms Control*, p. 40.

30 Bull, *Control of the Arms Race*, p. 66.

31 Lefever, *Arms*, p. xii.

32 King, 'Arms Control', p. 100.

33 Schelling and Halperin, *Strategy*, pp. 58–9.

34 Bull, *Control of the Arms Race*, p. xi.

35 Schelling and Halperin, *Strategy*, p. 77.

36 Lefever, *Arms*, p. xiii.

37 Schelling and Halperin, *Strategy*, p. 5.

38 Lefever, *Arms*, p. xiii.

39 Schelling, 'Reciprocal Measures', p. 174.

40 Weisner, Foreword to Brennan, *Arms Control*, pp. 14–15.

41 Schelling and Halperin, *Strategy*, p. 34.

42 King, 'Arms Control', p. 100.

43 Schelling and Halperin, *Strategy*, p. 132.

44 Henry A. Kissinger, 'Why we must put our Intellectual House in Order,' in Lefever, *Arms*, p. 141.

...rin, *Strategy*, p. 134.

...must', p. 140.

...7.

...*ms Race*, p. 196.

...rements', p. 48.

...rms Control', p. 68.

54 Bull, *Control of the Arms Race*, p. 11.
55 Kissinger, 'Why we must', pp. 139–40.
56 Weisner, 'Arms Limitation', p. 199.
57 Bowie, 'Arms Control', p. 72.
58 Kissinger, 'Why we must', p. 145.
59 Schelling and Halperin, *Strategy*, p. 47.
60 Ibid., p. 91.
61 Ibid., p. 132.
62 Bowie, 'Basic Requirements', p. 49.
63 Fred Charles Ikle, 'After Detection – What?' in Lefever, *Arms*, p. 232.
64 Bowie, 'Basic Requirements', p. 47.
65 Schelling and Halperin, *Strategy*, p. 108.
66 Bowie, 'Basic Requirements', p. 48.
67 Ibid., p. 51.
68 Bull, *Control of the Arms Race*, p. 65.

Chapter 2   The Development of Arms Control

1 Richard Burt, 'International Security and the Relevance of Arms Control', paper presented to the 1980 Millennium Conference, London School of Economics, p. 21.
2 Reg Gadney, *Kennedy* (London, 1983), pp. 154–5.
3 William Manchester, *One Brief Shining Moment: Remembering Kennedy* (London, 1983), p. 205.
4 John F. Kennedy, *The Strategy of Peace* (New York, 1960), pp. 19–30.
5 See above, pp. 10–11.
6 Johan Jurgen Holst, 'On How to Achieve Progress in Nuclear Arms Negotiations', *Bulletin of Peace Proposals*, 16, 2 (1985), p. 92.
7 Marek Thee, 'Arms Control: The Retreat from Disarmament, the Record to Date and the Search for Alternatives', *Journal of Peace Research*, 14, 2 (1977), p. 96.
8 Richard H. Ullman, 'Nuclear Arms: How Big a Cut?', *New York Times Magazine*, 16 November 1986, p. 71.

9 Bernard Brodie, 'On Clarifying the Objectives of Arms Control', *ACIS Working Paper No. I* (Programme in Arms Control and International Security, UCLA, 1976), p. 3.

10 Joseph Kruzel, 'What's Wrong with the Traditional Approach?', *Washington Quarterly*, 8, 2 (Spring 1985), p. 131.

11 John Garnett, 'Disarmament and Arms Control Since 1945', in Laurence W. Martin (ed.), *Strategic Thought in the Nuclear Age*, (London, 1979), p. 217.

12 Thomas Schelling, 'What Went Wrong with Arms Control?', *Foreign Affairs*, Winter 1985–6, p. 224.

13 Ibid., p. 226.

14 Ibid., p. 229.

15 Garnett, 'Disarmament', p. 205.

16 Ibid.

17 Kruzel, 'What's Wrong', p. 128.

18 Andrew J. Pierre, 'The Diplomacy of SALT', *International Security*, 5 (Summer 1980), p. 192. See also Kruzel, 'What's Wrong', p. 128.

19 Ibid., p. 128.

20 Holst, 'How to Achieve Progress', pp. 90–1.

21 Garnett, 'Disarmament', p. 194.

22 Christoph Bertram, 'Arms Control and Technological Change: Elements of a New Approach', *Adelphi Paper 146* (London, 1978), pp. 15–31.

23 Stephen J. Flanagan, 'SALT II: The Arms Control Process Unravels', in Albert Carnesale (ed.), *Learning from Experience with Arms Control*, Report submitted to US ACDA, (JFK School of Government, Harvard University, Boston, 1986), p. 5/47.

24 *Washington Post*, 27 June 1972.

25 Gallup Poll, cited in Tom W. Smith, 'The Polls: American Attitudes Toward the Soviet Union and Communism', *Public Opinion Quarterly*, 47, 2 (Summer 1983), p. 280.

26 NBC/AP Poll, February 1979, cited in Sean M. Lynn-Jones, 'Lulling and Stimulating Effects of Arms Control', in Carnesale, *Learning from Experience* p. 7/47.

27 Pierre, 'Diplomacy', p. 179.

28 Zbigniew Brzezinski, 'From Arms Control to Controlled Security', *Wall Street Journal*, 10 July 1984. See also Kruzel, 'What's Wrong', p. 124.

29 Eugene Rostow, 'The Case Against SALT II', *Commentary* (February 1979), p. 25. Similar arguments were advanced by John F. Lehman (later President Reagan's Secretary of the Navy) and Seymour Weiss, *Beyond the SALT II Failure* (New York, 1981), p. 8.

30 Joseph Kruzel, 'From Rush–Bagot to START: The Lessons of Arms Control', *Orbis*, 30, 1 (Spring 1986), p. 212.

31 Schelling, 'What Went Wrong', p. 224.

32 Kruzel, 'What's Wrong', p. 130.
33 Richard Burt, 'Defence Policy and Arms Control: Defining the Problem',
    in R. Burt (ed.), *Arms Control and Defence Postures in the 1980's* (London,
    1982), p. 5.
34 Burt, 'International Security', p. 4.
35 Michael Krepon, *Strategic Stalemate: Nuclear Weapons and Arms Control in
    American Politics* (London, 1984), p. 134.

Chapter 3   Arms Control and Technological Change

 1 Andrew J. Pierre, 'The Diplomacy of SALT', *International Security*, 5, 1
    (Summer 1980), p. 192.
 2 Lord Zuckerman, *Science Advisers, Scientific Advisers and Nuclear Weapons*
    (London, 1980), p. 11.
 3 Knud S. Larsen, 'Social Psychological Factors in Military Technology
    and Strategy', *Journal of Peace Research*, 23, 4 (December 1986), p. 391.
 4 For example, Michael Krepon, *Strategic Stalemate: Nuclear Weapons and Arms
    Control in American Politics* (London, 1984), p. 128.
 5 A survey of various motivations for state acquisition of military
    capabilities can be found in Michael Sheehan, *The Arms Race* (Oxford,
    1983), ch. 1.
 6 Graham T. Allison and Frederick A. Morris, 'Armaments and Arms
    Control: Exploring the Determinants of Military Weapons', in Franklin
    A. Long and George Rathjens (eds), *Arms, Defence Policy and Arms Control*
    (New York, 1975), p. 118.
 7 Harvey Brooks, 'The Military Innovation System and the Qualitative
    Arms Race', in Long and Rathjens, *Arms*, p. 77.
 8 Jack Anderson, 'Pentagon Invades Buck Rogers' Turf,' *Washington Post*,
    9 January 1981.
 9 Zuckerman, *Science Advisers*, p. 11.
10 Robert S. McNamara, 'Address to UPI Editors', San Francisco, 18
    September 1967.
11 Robert Perry, *The Interaction of Technology and Doctrine in the USAF*, RAND
    Paper P6281 (Santa Monica, Ca, 1979), p. 1.
12 Ibid., p. 4.
13 Allison and Morris, 'Armaments', p. 108.
14 Ibid., pp. 104–5.
15 Herbert F. York, 'Military Technology and National Security', *Scientific
    American*, 221, 2 (August 1969), p. 27.
16 M. T. Gallagher and K. F. Spielmann, *Soviet Decision-Making for Defence*
    (New York, 1972), p. 8.
17 Ibid., p. 9.

18 Allison and Morris, 'Armaments', p. 119.
19 John Foster, Testimony to US Senate, 90th Congress, 2nd Session, Committee on Armed Services, Preparedness Investigating Sub-committee, *Status of U.S. Strategic Power, Hearings* (Washington, DC, 1968), p. 12.
20 Herbert York, *Race to Oblivion* (New York, 1970), pp. 234–5.
21 Deborah Shapley, 'Technology Creep and the Arms Race: Two Future Arms Control Problems,' *Science*, 202 (20 October 1978), p. 292.
22 Allison and Morris, 'Armaments', p. 49.
23 *Investigation of the Preparedness Program*, Report by the Preparedness Investigating Sub-committee, Committee on Armed Services, US Senate, 90th Congress, 2nd Session (Washington, DC, 1968), p. 17.
24 Gerard M. Smith, *Doubletalk* (New York, 1980), p. 472.
25 Zuckerman, *Science Advisers*, p. 5.
26 Smith, *Doubletalk*, p. 154.
27 Dr John Foster, cited in James R. Kurth, 'Why We Buy the Weapons We Do,' *Foreign Policy*, 11 (Summer 1973), p. 48.
28 Zuckerman, *Science Advisers*, p. 11.
29 This study of the Trident decision follows that the John Steinbrunner and Barry Carter, 'Organisational and Political Dimensions of the Strategic Posture: The Problems of Reform', in Long and Rathjens, *Arms*, pp. 133–42.
30 Allison and Morris, 'Armaments', p. 126.
31 Ibid., p. 102.
32 Robert C. Herold and Shane E. Mahoney, 'Military Hardware Procurement: Some Comparative Observations on Soviet and American Policy Processes', *Comparative Politics*, 6, 4 (July 1974), p. 598.
33 Frank J. Gaffney, Jr, 'New Weapons Technology: The Challenge for Arms Control', in William T. Parsons (ed.), *Arms Control and Strategic Stability* (Lenham, Maryland, 1986), p. 41.
34 Bruce D. Berkowitz, 'Technological Progress, Strategic Weapons and American Nuclear Policy', *Orbis*, 29, 2 (Summer 1985), p. 254.
35 Robert Kennedy, 'New Weapons Technologies: Implications for Defence Policy', *Parameters*, 9, 2 (June 1979), p. 65.
36 Robert Handberg and Robert Bledsoe, 'Shifting Patterns in the American Military Budget Process: An Overview', *Journal of Strategic Studies*, December 1979, p. 355.
37 Ted Greenwood, *Making the MIRV: A Study of Defence Decision-Making* (Cambridge, Mass., 1975), p. 393.
38 Allison and Morris, 'Armaments', p. 121.
39 Kurth, 'Why We Buy', p. 42.
40 *Congressional Quarterly*, Weekly Report, 35, 28 (9 July 1977), p. 1405.
41 Herold and Mahoney, 'Military Hardware Procurement', p. 598.
42 Edward L. Warner, III, 'Soviet Strategic Force Posture: Some Alternative Explanations', in Frank B. Horton, Anthony C. Rogerson and

Edward L. Warner, III (eds), *Comparative Defense Policy* (Baltimore, 1974), p. 311.

43 Directorate of Intelligence, *The Soviet Weapons Industry: An Overview* (CIA, Langley, Va, 1986), p. 5.

44 Stan Woods, *Weapons Acquisition in the Soviet Union* (ASIDES No. 24, Centre for Defence Studies, University of Aberdeen, Summer 1982), p. 42.

45 Arthur J. Alexander, 'Weapons Acquisition in the Soviet Union, the United States and France', in Horton et al., *Comparative Defense Policy*, p. 432.

46 Woods, *Weapons Acquisition*, p. 53.

47 David Holloway, 'The Soviet Style of Military R and D', in Franklin A. Long and Judith Reppy (eds), *The Genesis of New Weapons* (New York, 1980), p. 155.

48 Warner, 'Soviet Strategic Force Posture', p. 314.

49 Woods, *Weapons Acquisition*, p. 32.

50 Arthur J. Alexander, *Soviet Science and Weapons Acquisition*, RAND-2492-NAS (Santa Monica, Ca, 1982), p. 18.

51 Jack Manno, *Arming the Heavens: The Hidden Military Agenda for Space. 1945–1975* (New York, 1984), p. 13.

52 William J. Broad, 'Star Wars Traced to Eisenhower Era', *New York Times*, 18 October 1986.

53 Quoted in Robert E. Hunter, 'SDI: Return to Basics', *Washington Quarterly*, Winter 1985, p. 155.

54 Shapley, 'Technology Creep', p. 291.

55 For example, Larsen, 'Social Psychological Factors', p. 127.

56 Zuckerman, *Science Advisers*, p. 5.

57 Berkowitz, 'Technological Progress', p. 252.

58 Gallagher and Spielmann, *Soviet Decision-Making*, p. 5.

59 Smith, Doubletalk, p. 190.

Chapter 4   Economic Implications of Arms Control

1 Emile Benoit, 'The Economic Impact of Disarmament in the United States', in Seymour Melman (ed.), *Disarmament: Its Politics and Economics* (Boston, Mass., 1962), p. 136.

2 Bernard Brodie, *How Much is Enough? Guns versus Butter Revisited*, California Seminar on Arms Control and Foreign Policy (Santa Monica, Ca, 1975), p. 1.

3 For example, Major Stephen H. Russell, USAF, 'Defense Spending and Economic Health', *Air Force Magazine*, April 1982 pp. 64–5.

4 For example, R. Huisken, 'Armaments and Development', in H. Tuomi and R. Vayrynen (eds), *Militarisation and Arms Production* (London, 1982), pp. 24–5.

5 Seymour Harris, 'Can We Prosper Without Arms?', *Survival*, 2 (1960), p. 3.

6 Economist Intelligence Unit, *The Economic Effects of Disarmament* (London, 1963), p. 124.

7 Pierre Arcq, 'Reconversion', *Peace News*, 14 September 1979, p. 9.

8 J. P. Dunne and R. P. Smith, *The Economic Consequences of Reduced U.K. Military Expenditure*, Birkbeck College Discussion Paper No. 144 (London, 1983), p. 10.

9 Benoit, 'Economic Impact', p. 146.

10 UN Department of Economic and Social Affairs, *Economic Consequences of Disarmament* (New York, 1962), para. 176.

11 Roy Mason, *Hansard*, 3 February 1975. Quoted in D. Smith, 'Principles of a Conversion Programme', in D. Elliott et al., *Alternative Work For Military Industries* (London, 1977), p. 29.

12 Goran Lindgren, 'Armaments and Economic Performance in Industrialized Market Economies', *Journal of Peace Research*, 21, 4 (1984), p. 380.

13 Employment Research Associates, *The Empty Pork Barrel* (1982), quoted in J. J. Joseph, 'The Economic Impact of Military Spending', in P. Joseph and S. Rosenblum (eds), *Search for Sanity* (Boston, Mass., 1984), p. 253.

14 Although Stephen H. Russell ('Defense Spending', p. 65) has claimed that defence industries are *more* labour intensive than civilian counterparts, the overwhelming weight of evidence contradicts this view.

15 *New York Times*, 17 September 1982.

16 Cited in T. Webb, *The Arms Drain: Job Risk and Industrial Decline* (London, 1982), p. 15.

17 Dunne and Smith, *Economic Consequences*, p. 18.

18 Robert De Grasse, Jr, Paul Murphy and William Roger, 'The Costs and Consequences of Reagan's Military Build-Up' (Council on Economic Priorities, 1982), quoted in J. J. Joseph, 'The Economic Impact', p. 253.

19 Seymour Melman, 'The Conversion of Military Economy: The USSR', in Lloyd J. Dumas (ed.), *The Political Economy of Arms Reduction* (Boulder, Colorado, 1982), p. 70.

20 Benoit, 'The Economic Impact', p. 151.

21 Reijo Lindroos, 'Disarmament, Employment and the Western Trade Unions', *Current Research on Peace and Violence*, 3, 2 (1980), p. 5.

22 Seymour Melman, 'Problems of Conversion from Military to Civilian Economy', *Bulletin of Peace Proposals*, 16, 1 (1985), p. 12.

23 Ibid.

24 Lloyd Dumas, 'Converting the Military Economy', in Joseph and Rosenblum, *Search for Sanity*, p. 553.

25 D. Smith, 'Community Planning and Base Conversion,' in D. Elliott et al., *Alternative Work*, p. 59.

26 Government of California, '*The Potential Transfer of Skills from Defence to Non-Defence Industries* (Sacramento, Ca, 1968), cited in D. Smith, 'Principles of a Conversion Programme', p. 29.
27 Lloyd Dumas, 'Converting the Military Economy', p. 541.
28 Benoit, 'The Economic Impact', p. 148.
29 Emile Benoit, 'Growth Effects of Defence in Developing Countries', *International Development Review*, 14, 1 (January 1972), pp. 2–10.
30 United Nations Organisation, *Economic and Social Effects of the Armaments Race and Its Extremely Harmful Effects on World Peace and Security* (Document A/37/386, New York, 1982), p. 41.
31 A. Cappelen, N. P. Gleditsch and O. Bjerkholt, 'Military Spending and Economic Growth in the O.E.C.D. Countries', *Journal of Peace Research*, 21, 4 (1984), p. 362.
32 D. Dabelko and J. McCormick, 'Opportunity Costs of Defence: Some Cross-National Evidence,' *Journal of Peace Research*, 14, 2 (1977), p. 153.
33 Cited in Russell, 'Defense Spending', p. 65.
34 Ibid., p. 62.
35 Steve Chan, 'The Impact of Defence Spending on Economic Performance: A Survey of Evidence and Problems', *Orbis*, 29, 2 (1985), p. 413.
36 R. Huisken, 'Armaments', p. 13.
37 Cappelen et al., 'Military Spending', p. 372.
38 *Economist*, 8 September 1956.
39 Dunne and Smith, *Economic Consequences*, p. 8.
40 Martin Walker, 'Britannia's Self-Inflicted Wound', *Guardian*, 25 April 1983.
41 Ibid.
42 Lloyd J. Dumas, 'The Impact of the Military Budget on the Domestic Economy', *Current Research on Peace and Violence*, Vol 3 (1980), p. 75.
43 Bruce M. Russett, *What Price Vigilance?* (New Haven, Conn., 1970), p. 134.
44 See, for example, Mikhail Gorbachev's interview in the Czech Party Newspaper, quoted in Mikhail Gorbachev, '*For a Nuclear Free World*' (Moscow, 1987), p. 175.
45 V. Aboltin, 'Razoruzhenie: ekonomichesk: slaborazvytye strany', *Narody Azii: afriki*, 4 (1962), p. 20. Quoted in Joseph L. Wieczynski, 'Economic Consequences of Disarmament: The Soviet View', *Russian Review*, 27, 3 (July 1968), p. 280.
46 Ibid., p. 276.
47 Samuel B. Payne, Jr, 'The Soviet Debate on Strategic Arms Limitation: 1968–72', *Soviet Studies*, 27, 1 (1975), p. 42.
48 Ibid., p. 36.
49 Lloyd J. Dumas, 'Disarmament and Economy in Advanced Industrialised Countries – The U.S. and the U.S.S.R.', *Bulletin of Peace Proposals*, 12, 1 (1981), p. 7.

50 M. Rubinstein, 'Economic Consequences of General and Complete Disarmament', *New Times*, 29 (18 July 1962), p. 10.
51 Lloyd J. Dumas, 'Disarmament and Economy', p. 9.
52 See ch. 1, p. 18.
53 *Department of State Bulletin*, 17 July 1972, p. 80.
54 R. George, 'The Economics of Arms Control,' *International Security*, 3 (1978), p. 96.
55 Congressional Budget Office, *SALT and the U.S. Stragetic Forces Budget* (Washington, DC, 1976), p. 6.
56 *Aerospace Daily*, 16 July 1979.
57 Kevin N. Lewis, *The Economics of SALT Revisited* (Santa Monica, Ca, 1979), p. 28.
58 For example, Senator Nunn of Georgia, 'Nunn Ties Vote on SALT II to More Spending on Arms', *Baltimore Sun*, 26 July 1979.
59 'Proxmire says SALT II May Cost U.S. $100 Billion or More in New Weapons', *Washington Post*, 6 July 1979.
60 For example, Senator Metzenbaum, *Philadelphia Enquirer*, 4 August 1979.
61 Kenneth E. Boulding, 'Economic Implications of Arms Control', in Donald G. Brennan (ed.), *Arms Control, Disarmament and National Security* (New York, 1961), p. 153.
62 Ibid., p. 154.
63 Donald G. Brennan, 'Setting and Goals of Arms Control', in Brennan, *Arms Control*, p. 40.

Chapter 5 Talking to Yourself

1 John Newhouse, *Cold Dawn: The Story of SALT* (New York, 1973), p. 231.
2 Stephen E. Miller, 'Politics over Promise: The Domestic Impediments to Arms Control', *International Security*, 8, 4 (Spring 1984), p. 68.
3 Raymond Garthoff, 'Negotiating with the Russians: Some Lessons From SALT', *International Security*, 1, 4 (Spring 1977), p. 4.
4 Ibid., p. 19.
5 Jimmy Carter, *Keeping Faith* (London, 1982), p. 218.
6 Richard Strout, 'Views from Backstage', *The New Republic*, 18 April 1983, p. 39.
7 Miller, 'Politics over Promise', p. 69.
8 Statement of Robert W. Buchheim, *Arms Control in Outer Space*. Hearings Before the Sub-committee on International Security and Scientific Affairs, House Foreign Affairs Committee (Washington, DC, 1984), p. 130.
9 Andrew J. Pierre, 'The Diplomacy of SALT', *International Security*, 5, 1 (Summer 1980), p. 193.

10　Richard Burt, 'Defence Policy and Arms Control: Defining the Problem', in R. Burt (ed.), *Arms Control and Defence Postures in the 1980's* (London, 1982), p. 5.

11　Marvin Kalb and Bernard Kalb, *Kissinger* (Boston, Mass., 1974), p. 112.

12　Quoted in Duncan Clarke, *Politics of Arms Control* (New York 1979), p. 32.

13　Quoted in Alan Platt, *The U.S. Senate and Strategic Arms Policy 1969–1977*, (Boulder, Colorado, 1978), p. 14.

14　Gerard Smith, *Doubletalk* (New York, 1980), p. 164.

15　Ibid., p. 443.

16　*Congressional Quarterly*, 15 June 1974, p. 1546. Richard Perle, Jackson's assistant, insisted in 1976 that Jackson and he were not behind the 1972 purge. The Washington rumour mill had no doubts, however.

17　Anatol Rapoport, *Conflict in Man-Made Environment* (Harmondsworth, 1974), p. 213.

18　Miller, 'Politics over Promise', p. 87.

19　*Guardian*, 14 February 1978.

20　Phil Williams, 'The Senate and SALT II', paper presented to the 1979 Annual Conference of the British International Studies Association, p. 14.

21　Platt, *The U.S. Senate*, p. 14.

22　*Washington Post*, 22 March 1970. The Senate Foreign Relations Committee had voted to approve the Brooke Resolution the day before.

23　*Congressional Record*, 25 February 1976, p. S2289.

24　*Financial Times*, 25 May 1984 (House Vote) and 14 June 1984 (Senate Vote).

25　S. Schemann, 'Soviets Trying to Explain Arms Linkage Issue', *New York Times*, 17 October 1986.

26　Barry Blechman, 'Do Negotiated Arms Limitations Have a Future?', *Foreign Affairs*, 59, 1 (Autumn 1980), p. 106.

27　Garthoff, 'Negotiating with the Russians', p. 4.

28　Miller, 'Politics over Promise', p. 88.

29　Ibid., p. 87.

30　Bruce M. Russett, *What Price Vigilance?* (New Haven, Conn., 1970), p. 26.

31　Smith, *Doubletalk*, p. 461.

32　*Philadelphia Inquirer*, 4 August 1979.

33　Henry Kissinger, *The White House Years* (London, 1979), p. 1240.

34　Newhouse, *Cold Dawn*, p. 246.

35　William H. Baugh, *The Politics of Nuclear Balance* (London, 1984), p. 18.

36　Stephen M. Walt, 'Why Clever Schemes Don't Work', *Issues in Science and Technology*, 167, 2 (March 1986), p. 89.

37　Sverre Lodgaard, 'The Functions of SALT', *Journal of Peace Research*, 14, 1 (1977), p. 16.

38 Miller, 'Politics over Promise', p. 80.
39 Carter, Keeping Faith, p. 81.
40 Robert Bowie, 'The Bargaining Aspects of Arms Control: The SALT Experience', in William R. Kintner and Robert L. Pfaltzgraff, *SALT: Implications for Arms Control in the 1970's*, (Pittsburgh, 1973), p. 134.
41 Baroness Young, Minister of State in the Foreign and Commonwealth Office, in the House of Lords, 15 October 1986.
42 Presidential Statement, 27 May 1986.
43 *Des Moines Register*, 6 June 1986.
44 *New York Times*, 19 September 1986; *Baltimore Sun*, 20 October 1986.
45 Pierre Gallois, 'Space War Plans and Defense Strategy', *Politique Internationale*, Spring 1984, p. 185.
46 *The Times*, 17 May 1985, 12 March 1985, 11 February 1985, respectively.
47 Lloyd S. Takeshita, 'The Strategic Defence Initiative and NATO', *Military Review*, April 1986, p. 34.
48 *Guardian*, 13 December 1985.
49 Bernard D'Abeville, 'European Attitudes Towards the S.D.I.', quoted in Ivo D. Daalder and Lynn Page Whittaker, 'S.D.I's Implications for Europe: Strategy, Politics and Technology', in Stephen J. Flanagan and Fen Osler Hampson (eds), *Securing Europe's Future* (London, 1986), p. 42.
50 Hugh De Santis, 'S.D.I. and the European Allies: Riding the Tiger', *Arms Control Today*, 16, 2 (March 1986), p. 10.
51 *Washington Post*, 1 October 1986.
52 *The Milwaukee Journal*, 23 June 1986.
53 Miller, 'Politics over Promise', p. 83; see also Kissinger, *White House Years*, pp. 1232–3.
54 Gerald M. Steinberg, 'The Role of Process in Arms Control Negotiations', *Journal of Peace Research*, 22, 5 (1985), p. 266.
55 Ibid.
56 Theodore Sorenson, *Kennedy* (New York, 1965), p. 823.
57 Steinberg, 'Role of Process', p. 267.
58 Sorenson, *Kennedy*, p. 828.
59 Garthoff, 'Negotiating with the Russians', p. 22.
60 Henry Kissinger, *A World Restored*, (London, 1957), p. 326.

Chapter 6   Bargaining with the Adversary

1 Kevin N. Lewis, *The Economics of SALT Revisited* Santa Monica, Ca, 1979), p. 4.
2 Keijo Kerhonen, 'Disarmament Talks as an Instrument of International Politics', *Cooperation and Conflict*, 5 (1970), p. 152.

3 Sverre Lodgaard, 'The Functions of SALT', *Journal of Peace Research*, 14, 1 (1977), p. 16.

4 Michael Krepon, *Strategic Stalemate; Nuclear Weapons and Arms Control in American Politics* (London, 1984), p. 130.

5 Robert J. Einhorn, *Negotiating from Strength* (New York, 1985), p. 36.

6 Secretary of Defense James Schlesinger, '*Hearing on US–USSR Strategic Policies*, Sub-committee on Arms Control, International Law and Organisation, Senate Committee on Foreign Relations, 93rd Congress, 4 March 1974 (Washington, DC, 1974), p. 41.

7 Strobe Talbott, *Endgame: The Inside Story of SALT II* (New York, 1979), p. 52.

8 Marek Thee, 'Arms Control: The Retreat from Disarmament, The Record to Date and the Search for Alternatives', *Journal of Peace Research*, 14, 2 (1977), p. 103; see also Jane M. O. Sharp, 'MBFR as Arms Control', *Arms Control Today* (April 1976), pp. 1–3.

9 M. Sheehan and J. H. Wyllie, *The Economist Pocket Guide to Defence* (Oxford. 1986), pp. 29–30.

10 *Dallas Morning News*, 27 October 1986.

11 Vladimir Chernyshev, *Washington: A Policy of Eroding Treaties and Agreements* (Moscow, 1986), pp. 57–9.

12 Quoted in *Time* magazine, 27 October 1986, p. 37.

13 Raymond Garthoff, 'Negotiating with the Soviets: Some Lessons from SALT', *International Security*, 1, 4 (1977), p. 20.

14 Gerard Smith, *Doubletalk* (Doubleday, New York, 1980), p. 190.

15 Lodgaard, 'Functions of SALT', p. 10.

16 Einhorn, *Negotiating from Strength*, p. 44.

17 *Consideration of Mr. Paul C. Warnke to be Director of the U.S. Arms Control and Disarmament Agency and Ambassador*, Hearings, Committee on Armed Services, US Senate, 95th Congress, 1st Session (Washington, DC, 1977), p. 45.

18 Ibid., p. 192.

19 Einhorn, *Negotiating from Strength*, p. 107.

20 Einhorn's study (above) is an excellent survey of the intricacies and policy implications of this aspect of arms control negotiations.

21 This was the attitude of Senator Henry Jackson, a prominent conservative Democrat critic of arms control during the 1960s and 1970s. See, for example, H. Jackson quoted in *Arms Control and Disarmament*, Hearings before the Preparedness Investigating Sub-committee of the Committee on Armed Services, US Senate, 87th Congress, 2nd Session (Washington, DC, 1962), p. 90.

22 Garthoff, 'Negotiating with the Soviets', p. 13.

23 Christopher J. Makins, 'The Superpowers Dilemma: Negotiating in the Nuclear Age', *Survival*, 27, 4 (July–August 1985), p. 174.

24 Krepon, *Strategic Stalemate*, p. 91.

25 Einhorn, *Negotiating from Strength*, p. 71.

26 Ibid., p. 72.

27 Andrew J. Pierre, 'The Diplomacy of SALT', *International Security*, 5 (Summer 1980), p. 181.

28 Gerald M. Steinberg, 'The Role of Process in Arms Control Negotiations', *Journal of Peace Research*, 22, 3 (1985), p. 261. A similar view is put forward by Rip Bulkely, 'The Trouble with Nuclear Disarmament by Negotiations', *Bulletin of Peace Proposals*, 14, 4 (1983), p. 313.

29 Ibid.

30 See, for example, 'Disarmament Conference in Ancient China', in T. N. Dupuy and G. M. Hammerman (eds), *A Documentary History of Arms Control and Disarmament* (New York, 1973), pp. 3–4.

31 Bulkeley, 'Trouble with Nuclear Disarmament', p. 313.

32 T. Schelling and M. Halperin, *Strategy and Arms Control* (New York, 1961), p. 77.

33 F. Ikle, *How Nations Negotiate* (New York, 1964), p. 5.

34 Steinberg, 'Role of Process', p. 270.

35 Garthoff, 'Negotiating with the Soviets', pp. 16–17.

36 Einhorn, *Negotiating from Strength*, p. 58.

37 Garthoff, 'Negotiating with the Soviets', p. 21.

38 Robert Legvold, 'Strategic Doctrine and SALT: Soviet and American Views', *Survival*, 21, 1 (January–February 1979), p. 11.

39 Francois de Rose, 'European Concerns and SALT II', *Survival*, 21, 5 (September–October 1979), p. 206.

40 Garthoff, 'Negotiating with the Soviets', p. 5.

41 Steinberg, 'Role of Process', p. 268.

42 J. L. Nogee, 'Propaganda and Negotiations: The Case of the Ten Nation Disarmament Committee', *Journal of Conflict Resolution*, 7 (1963), p. 511.

43 Bulkeley, 'Trouble with Nuclear Disarmament', p. 315.

44 B. Blechman, 'Do Negotiated Arms Limitations Have a Future?' *Foreign Affairs*, 59, 1 (Autumn 1980), p. 106.

Chapter 7   The Verification of Agreements

1 Sidney Graybeal (US Representative on SALT Standing Consultative Commission, 1973–7), quoted in R. Scribner, T. J. Ralston and W. D. Metz, *The Verification Challenge* (Boston, 1985), p. 21.

2 George M. Seignious (ACDA Director) to Senate Foreign Relations Committee. *The SALT II Treaty Hearings, Part 2* (Washington, DC, 1979). p. 291.

3 Quoted in Richard Dean Burns, 'International Arms Inspection Policies Between World Wars 1919–1934.' *The Historian*, 31 (1969), p. 587.

4 Ibid., p. 592.

5 Quoted in William D. Jackson, 'Verification in Arms Control: Beyond NTM', *Journal of Peace Research*, 19, 4 (1982), p. 346.

6 Graybeal, quoted in Scribner et al., *The Verification Challenge*. Also *Pravda*, 13 May 1986, quoted in *Soviet News* (London), 14 May 1986, p. 235.

7 Freeman Dyson, 'Weapons and Hope', Part III, *New Yorker* (20 February 1983), p. 83.

8 *New York Times*, 11 February 1983.

9 *Pravda*, 13 May 1986, p. 235.

10 Stephen M. Meyer, 'Verification and Risk in Arms Control', *International Security*, 8, 4 (Spring 1984), p. 112.

11 Sir Geoffrey Johnson Smith, '*Draft General Report on the Future of Arms Control: Compliance and Verification Issues*', Military Committee of the North Atlantic Assembly, Document MC(85)5 (Brussels, April 1985), p. 8.

12 Fredric S. Feer, 'The Verification Problem: What it is and what could be done about it,' *Journal of Strategic Studies*, June 1985, p. 149.

13 Scribner et al., *The Verification Challenge*, p. 18.

14 A 1984 opinion poll carried out in the US found that 61 per cent of respondents believed that the Soviet Union had broken every treaty it had ever signed: *Christian Science Monitor*, 17 September 1984, cited in Mark M. Lowenthal, 'Verification: Soviet Compliance with Arms control Agreements', *Congressional Research Service Issue Brief No. 1B84131* (Washington, DC, May 1985), p. 9.

15 *Fundamentals of Nuclear Arms Control, Part IV, Treaty Compliance and Nuclear Arms control* (Washington, DC, June 1985), p. 22 (a report prepared by the Congressional Research Service for the Sub-committee on Arms Control, International Security and Science, of The House of Representatives Committee on Foreign Affairs).

16 See, for example, 'The President's Unclassified Report to the Congress on Soviet Non-Compliance with Arms Control Agreements', *Congressional Record*, 131 (March 1985), pp. S2530–S2530, in which President Reagan alledges the existence of a pattern of breaches of the ABM treaty indicating preparations for a nationwide Soviet defence.

17 *Military Implications of the Treaty on the Limitation of Strategic Offensive Arms and Protocol Thereto (SALT II Treaty)*, Vol I Committee on Armed Services, US Senate. (Washington, DC, 1979), p. 228.

18 Allan S. Krass, 'The Soviet View of Verification', in William C. Potter (ed.), *Verification and Arms Control* (Lexington, Mass., 1985), p. 55.

19 Michael Krepon, *Arms Control: Verification and Compliance.* (New York, 1984), p. 38.

20 Stephen M. Meyer, 'Verification', p. 113.

21 President Richard Nixon, instructions to SALT I negotiations team, quoted in Krepon, *Arms Control*, p. 17.
22 *The Defense Monitor*, 11, 8 (1982), p. 7.
23 Karl Pieragostini, 'Treaty Verification: Why?: How?: And How Much is Enough?', in P. Joseph and S. Rosenblum (eds.), *Search for Sanity* (Boston, Mass., 1984), p. 212.
24 *Verification of SALT II Agreement*, Special Report No. 56, US Department of State, Bureau of Public Affairs (Washington, DC, 1979), p. 6.
25 Richard Perle, 'What is Adequate Verification?', in Gordon J. Humphrey et al., *SALT II and American Security* (Cambridge, Mass., 1980), p. 53.
26 James A. Schear, 'Verifying Arms Agreements: Premises: Practices and Future Problems', in Ian A. Bellamy and Coit D. Blacker (eds), *The Verification of Arms Control Agreement* (London, 1983), p. 77.
27 Senator Larry Pressler, 'ASAT Ban Verification', *Baltimore Sun*, 20 June 1984, p. 19.
28 *Fundamentals of Nuclear Arms Control, Part IV*, p. 4.
29 Krepon, *Arms Control*, p. 8.
30 *Fiscal Year 1986 Arms Control Impact Statements* (Washington, DC, 1985) p. 354 (emphasis added).
31 Amron H. Katz, *Verification and SALT: The State of the Art and The Art of the State* (Washington, DC, 1979), p. 11.
32 Carnes Lord, 'Verification and the Future of Arms Control', *Strategic Review*, Spring 1978), p. 28.
33 In evidence to the Senate Foreign Relations Committee on 9 July 1979.
34 Those who argue that the verification technology is adequate include Congressman Les Aspin, 'The Verification of the SALT II Agreement', *Scientific American*, 240, 2 (February 1979), pp. 38–45: Philip J. Farley, 'Verification: On the Plus Side of the Salt II Balance Sheet', in William C. Potter (ed.), *Verification and SALT* (Boulder, Colorado, 1980), pp. 221–8; D. Hafmeister, J. Romm and K. Tsipis, 'The Verification of Compliance with Arms Control Agreements', *Scientific American*, 252, 3 (March 1985), p. 35 and US Congress, Senate Select Committee on Intelligence, *Principal Findings on the Capabilities of the US to Monitor the SALT II Treaty. Report* (Washington, DC, 1979).

Sceptics about the adequacy of the technology include Senator Jake Garn, 'The SALT II Verification Myth', *Strategic Review* 7, 3 (Summer 1979), pp. 16–24a; Amron Katz, 'The Fabric of Verification, the Warp and the Woof', in Potter (1980), *Verification*, pp. 193–220; and Congressman Jack Kemp, 'Congressional Expectations of SALT II', *Strategic Review*, 7, 1 (Winter 1979), pp. 16–25.
35 The categorization given here is that devised by William Jackson, 'Verification'. An alternative, though for obvious reasons, fairly similar, categorization is given in Karl Pieragostini, 'Treaty Verification'.

36 Aspin, 'The Verification', p. 37.

37 Krepon, *Arms Control*, p. 9.

38 Hafmeister et al., 'The Verification of Compliance', p. 29.

39 A very useful study of the value and limits of cooperative verification is given in James A. Schear, 'Co-operative Measures of Verification: How Necessary? How Effective?', in Potter (1985), *Verification*, pp. 7–35.

40 Mark M. Lowenthal, 'SALT II Verification: Outstanding Issues', *Congressional Research Service Issue Brief No. 1B79096* (Washington, DC, 1980), p. 6.

41 Meyer, 'Verification', p. 126.

42 Colonel R. Shearer, '*On-Site Inspection for Arms Control: Breaking the Verification Barrier*' (Washington, 1984), p. 16.

43 C. K. Allard, 'Intelligence and Arms Control; Process and Priorities' *Fletcher Forum*, Winter 1981, p. 21.

44 W. Slocombe, 'Verification and Negotiation', in Stephen E. Miller (ed.), *The Nuclear Weapon Freeze and Arms Control* (New York, 1984).

45 Meyer, 'Verification', p. 125.

46 *The SALT II Treaty Hearings*, Part 2, p. 508.

47 Ibid., Part 1, p. 508.

48 ACDA Director-Designate, Eugene Rostow, to Senate Foreign Relations Committee, 24 July 1981.

49 For example, S. B. Payne, Jr, *The Soviet Union and SALT* (Cambridge, Mass., 1980), p. 81.

50 R Zheleznov, 'Monitoring Arms Limitation Measures', *International Affairs* (Moscow), July 1982, p. 75.

51 R. Timerbayev, *Problems of Verification*, (Moscow, 1984).

52 Ibid., p. 7.

53 Moscow World Service in English, 8 October 1983, quoted in Charles R. Gellner, 'Soviet Positions on Compliance With and Verification of Arms Control Agreements' (unpublished paper, Washington, DC, 1985), p. 29.

54 Allan S. Krass, 'The Soviet View of Verification', p. 37. This chapter is an excellent survey of the topic.

55 Charles R. Gellner, 'Verification Issues in Europe, Including the Attitude of the Warsaw Pact', in John O'Manique (ed.), *A Proxy for Trust: Views on the Verification Issue in Arms Control and Disarmament Negotiations* (Ottawa, 1985), p. 33.

56 See, for example, *Sovetskaya Rossiya*, 29 January 1986, p. 5.

57 Zheleznov, 'Monitoring Arms Limitation', p. 75.

58 *Arms Control Agreements: Message Transmitting a Report on Soviet Noncompliance with Arms Control Agreements*, House Document No. 98–158 (Washington, DC, 1984), p. 5.

59 SALT II Treaty, in Arms Control and Disarmament Agency, *Arms Control and Disarmament Agreements. Texts and Histories of Negotiations* (Washington, DC, 1982), p. 266.

60 S. A. Cohen, 'The Evolution of Soviet Views on Verification', in Potter (1980), *Verification*, p. 51.

61 James A. Schear, 'Arms Control Treaty Compliance: Buildup to a Breakdown?', *International Security*, 10, 2 (Autumn 1985), 148.

62 Sidney N. Graybeal and Michael Krepon, 'The Standing Consultative Commission', *International Security*, 10, 2 (Autumn 1985), p. 186.

63 Zheleznov, 'Monitoring Arms Limitation', p. 76.

64 *Sovetskaya Rossiya*, 29 January 1986, p. 5.

65 Strobe Talbot, *Endgame: The Inside Story of SALT II* (New York, 1979), 98.

66 WTO, 'Prague Declaration' of 5 January 1983.

67 See, for example, Barry M. Blechman, 'The Comprehensive Test Ban Negotiations', *Arms Control Today*, 11, 5 (June 1981), p. 3.

68 *International Herald Tribune*, 28 July 1983, p. 3.

69 Jackson, 'Verification', p. 346.

70 Graybeal, quoted in Scribner et al., *The Verification Challenge*, p. 21.

71 Krepon, *Arms Control*, p. 40.

72 Glen Buchan, 'The Verification Spectrum', *Bulletin of the Atomic Scientists*, November 1983, p. 16.

73 Ibid.

74 A phrase used by Congressman Dante B. Fascell, Chairman of the House Foreign Affairs Committee. *Congressional Record*, (11 October 1984), p. E4482, col. 1.

75 'SALT I Compliance and SALT II Verification', *Selected Documents No. 7*, US Department of State, Bureau of Public Affairs (Washington, DC, 1978, p. 12.

76 US Defence Intelligence felt Krasnoyarsk was an illegal ABM radar. The CIA was unsure but felt it was poorly designed for the task if such was its role, while British Intelligence concluded in January 1985 that Krasnoyarsk was 'unlikely' to serve an ABM function. Michael Gordon, 'CIA is skeptical that New Soviet Radar is Part of an ABM Defence System', *National Journal* 9 March 1985, p. 524.

77 Jeannette Voas, 'The Arms Control Compliance Debate,' *Survival*, 28, 1 (January–February 1986), p. 28.

78 Krepon, *Arms Control*, p. 50.

79 L. Freedman, 'Assured Detection: Needs and Dysfunctions of Verification', in U. Nerlich (ed.), *The Western Panacea: Constraining Soviet Power Through Negotiation*, vol. 2 (Cambridge, Mass., 1984), p. 254.

80 Ambrose Bierce, *The Devil's Dictionary* (1911: Dover Publications edition, New York, 1958), p. 98.

81 Meyer, 'Verification', p. 122.
82 Voas, 'Arms Control', p. 28.
83 Meyer, 'Verification', p. 126.

Chapter 8   The Politics of Arms Control

1 Joseph Kruzel, 'From Rush–Bagot to START: The Lessons of Arms Control', *Orbis*, 30, (Spring 1986), p. 202.
2 Leslie H. Gelb, 'A Glass Half-Full', *Foreign Policy* 36 (Autumn 1979), p. 21.
3 Stephen J. Flanagan, 'SALT II: The Arms Control Process Unravels', in Albert Carnesale (ed.), *Learning From Experience with Arms Control*, Report Submitted to ACDA (John F. Kennedy School of Government, Harvard University, September 1986), p. 5/32.
4 Richard Burt, 'Defence Policy and Arms Control: Defining the Problem', in R. Burt (ed.), *Arms Control and Defence Postures in the 1980's* (London, 1982), p. 12.
5 Joseph Biden, 'The Five Myths of Reagan Arms Control', *Arms Control Today*, 16, 7 (October 1986), p. 5.
6 Kruzel, 'From Rush–Bagot to START') p. 201.
7 Ivo Daalder, 'The Limited Test-Ban Treaty', in Carnesale, *Learning from Experience*, p. 2/57.
8 Michael Howard, 'Is Arms Control Really Necessary?' (London, 1985), p. 3.
9 Ibid., p. 5.
10 Adam Garfinkle, *Orbis*, 29, 2 (Summer 1985), p. 277.
11 Howard, 'Arms Control', p. 15.
12 Michael McGuire, 'Deterrence: The Problem – Not the Solution', *Journal of Strategic Studies*, 9, 4 (December 1986), p. 36.
13 Gelb, 'A Glass Half-Full', p. 23.
14 *Guardian*, 2 June 1987.
15 *Daily Telegraph*, 29 April 1987.
16 Gerard Smith, *Doubletalk*, (Doubleday, New York, 1980), p. 72.
17 Mikhail Gorbachev, speech on Soviet television, 14 October 1986, in Mikhail Gorbachev, *For A Nuclear-Free World* (Moscow, 1987), p. 222.
18 Johan Jurgan Holst, 'On How To Achieve Progress in Nuclear Arms Negotiations', *Bulletin of Peace Proposals*, 16, 2 (1985), p. 87.
19 Mikhail Gorbachev, Political Report of the CPSU Central Committee, 25 February 1986, in Gorbachev, *Nuclear-Free World*, p. 39.
20 Mikhail Gorbachev, statement on Soviet television, 18 August 1986, in Gorbachev, *Nuclear-Free World*, p. 152.

21 Lawrence Freedman, 'Arms Control: On the Possibilities for a Second Coming', paper presented at the 1980 Millennium Conference, London School of Economics, p. 16.

22 Holst, 'How to Achieve Progress', p. 95.

23 Kruzel, 'From Rush–Bagot to START', p. 216.

Index